...DY IN OUR EVERYDAY LIVES
The Role of Popular Culture

TRAGEDY IN OUR EVERYDAY LIVES
The Role of Popular Culture

John Astley

This monograph is published by EDSERS 2022
www.edsers.co.uk

ISBN 978-1-915292-49-0

Designed and typeset by Copyrite, Exmouth
Printed by Biddles Books, King's Lynn

Other recent books by John Astley

Liberation & Domestication: Young People,
Youth Policy and Cultural Creativity. 2005

Culture and Creativity: The Beatles and Other Essays. 2006

Professionalism and Practice: Culture, Values and Service. 2006

Why Don't We Do It In The Road? The Beatles Phenomenon. 2006

Herbivores & Carnivores: The Struggle for
Democratic Cultural Values in post-War Britain. 2008

Access to Eden: The Rise and Fall of Public Sector Housing Ideals. 2010

Access to Eden: An Essay on Arts & Crafts values, Garden City ideals, and
the 'Wheatley' Housing Act of 1924. 2012 (An enlarged second edition)

The Role of Social Science in the Education
of Professional Practitioners. 2018

The Littleham Council Housing Estate. 2020

Sounds Good For Us: An Essay on Music and Everyday Life. 2020

Acknowledgements

I am grateful to a number of people for their helpful ideas and suggestions for this essay. However, special thanks must go to Rebecca Hillman for her conversations and comments.

Thanks also to Rachel and Chris Hills for reading and commenting on an early draft.

Contents

An Introduction

In this essay I wish to explore the idea of tragedy as proposed and discussed over many years since the Greeks of antiquity, and the ways in which the creative products of popular culture self-consciously use tragedy as a central motif in the stories being told about everyday life and the human condition, including suffering, a constant companion for social beings.

'Reality gives pain. That is why we remove from consciousness so many of our responses to it. Reality makes us feel guilty, and so arouses anxiety. To be reminded of reality renews the guilt feelings and the anxiety. Therefore, a direct reminder in art would be unwelcome: one would not find pleasure in the pain.' (Bentley 1965 p.258)

Indeed, one dimension of our 'tragic hero' is the determination not to give up in the face of the most dire circumstances, to carry on regardless of the fate that awaits us.

Hence, such a key challenge for the dramatist, and especially so the tragedian.

This call to take action, experienced by most of us, to respond to the travails of everyday life, to say something, leads to writing and performance; but also relates to the tragic events that are seen on our TV screens in news bulletins and documentary programmes. As TV viewers we have become used to watching recognisably tragic events around the world, like famines, the collateral damage on civilians from wars of many kinds, and the plight of refugees. As Stephanie Baker points out in her book 'Social Tragedy' (2017), TV coverage of such tragic events, this suffering brought to our domestic domain, has 'proposed' that we feel the need to respond to suffering as a legitimate social concern. So, as spectators of the many horrors of everyday life, we could be encouraged to become participants in a call for moral action. We can also see the links between what we see on the TV screen and the work of charities like Oxfam to both raise awareness and money. One well known response to such tragic events was Live Aid in July 1985, a popular culture response that did engage large numbers of people, and forced itself on to the foreign aid agenda, with both mixed motives and outcomes. Another populist moment for our politicians. There are of course questions raised about 'disaster fatigue', and there has been a good deal of discussion about the long term benefits of money related giving as a response to such tragic events. (for example see Rob Reich 'Just Giving' 2020) Responding to tragic events at home and abroad can stimulate some empathy, and the desire to be charitable. But, can greater long term benefits be achieved by going beyond donations, to engagement, to challenging the economic and political organisation of everyday life, that can be seen to create the circumstances of tragic events around the world?

I argue in this essay that our everyday popular cultures can indeed embrace these tragic events through the creative skills of writers and performers of Tragedy, enabling through drama the opportunity for us all to consider our own motivations and values. This has happened in our pasts, and it can happen again now in our contemporary lives. I shall be discussing the myriad nature of the artistic process as one of the best opportunities we now have (still have) to develop agency for people and their diverse culture groups, in order that we all have a voice.

However, while embarking on a discussion about tragedy, I shall also have to address comedy. Given the yin and yang nature of our everyday lives, of tears and laughter, the inter-relation between these emotional states cannot be ignored. Dramatic performance, and the creative arts in general show us that the inevitability of death is a constant source of laughter. Since ancient times the closeness of the dramatic masks Thalia for happy and Melpomene for sad, reminds of this dialectic relation.

And;
'Tragedy and comedy are concerned, as melodrama and farce are not, with

2

justice.' (Bentley 1965 p.260)

The link between tragedy and comedy emphasises that what we consider to be stable and secure is in fact vulnerable via often surprising tragic events, and, the comedic emphasis to laugh at ourselves in all our ridiculous, pompous and absurd ways. Our emotions are all in play! Irony plays a key part here, stuff happening to us, for unfathomable reasons, that we just do not understand, did not see coming. The 'audience' meanwhile have been let in to our destiny. We may be alone, even lonely, but we are being observed, our pain and pathos witnessed, and as I have said above, usually via TV.

Samuel Becket's theatre drew on this situation to great effect, absurdity and self-mockery, while waiting for Godot to turn up and restore order.

We must also acknowledge differences of opinion about why Tragedy is in our lives. Do we need Tragedy as a dramatic form to describe and even explain the human condition, especially so perhaps in the contemporary context?

But, also, are tragic events of life always with us, and do we need to deal with it as best as we can; talk about it in one form or another? Does engaging with the dramatic form, Tragedy, make us more aware of injustice and the 'fickle finger of fate'? These are key issues that will be addressed in this essay. In 1961 George Steiner announced the death of tragedy, primarily because he argued that tragedy could not exist in a rational society. Tragedy, he said was the child of irrationality, and that western civilisation had stopped all that chaotic and anarchic nonsense. I think that by the end of his life in 2020, even he thought there might be a role for dramatic tragedy, if the great loss of nerve by playwrights and their associates could be recovered? Of course Steiner's early 1960s argument came at a time when postmodern arguments were more commonplace, with for example the idea that the Modernist project, with a focus on a secure shared and imposed set of values, had come to an end. Culture was up for grabs!

I shall return later to consider Tragedy and Comedy in more detail, but for now my focus is on TV, as one dimension of popular culture, and as a vehicle for the dramatic form of Tragedy.

The Role of TV in society

Given what I said about why we have Tragedy, one of the key issues in this essay is my contention that tragic drama can play a valuable part in our everyday lives, and that the existing and conventional media forms, like TV, are more than able to fill this role. However, I do have to acknowledge that the tension between aesthetic, and for my argument, political aims, are going to come up against commercial aims. Of course this conflict of interests and controls does not just apply to TV, the same tensions are to be found right across the arts. The greater reliance on sponsorship in recent years also raises many concerns about for prospective creators and audiences; should we be associating with these people?

I also have to face the issue of the future that I have hoped for above, specifically so a vision for a better, more socially just future. Tragic drama can and does show us the ills of our current times, while frequently drawing on the tragic lives and events from the past. But, the loss of an alternative vision of the future must be addressed, partly as a critique of what is currently on offer, even social policy pronouncements. Can this vision of a better future, the good society, be put on the TV screen, or the cinema screen, or in music, etcetera? A vision for the future that includes real democratic relations that people will recognise as part of their world, understand, and want to embrace, or in other words, will this 'future' be an inclusive one? Will the people who have day to day control of TV scheduling, programming and commissioning, allow such access? These are some of the 'political' questions I shall be posing in this essay. Can popular cultures, especially TV, adequately address the issue of Utopian ideas, and not just on BBC4?

Throughout this essay I will be discussing the differences that exist on a daily basis between TV watching, and access to, and use of, arts facilities like galleries, museums, live music events of all genres, and the theatre. TV, whether broadcast live, or recorded, sits between live theatre and cinema, and also compared to these two is primarily accessed in the domestic domain. There are also some key issues here around social class, social status (including the dominance of Whiteness and Maleness), and educational experience, and I will be considering these matters in relation to my specific interest in TV drama, both its production and consumption.

We also have to face some key questions about the 'value' of TV, to both individuals, and 'the nation'. TV is both ephemeral and democratic in the widest senses, and given the constant attempt by free marketers to break up the BBC and Channel 4, these issues matter.

'Television was the medium through which working-class people were most likely to find out about what was being said about them. Commercial television (from 1955) was aggressively "popular"' (Sinfield 1989 p.269)

As I shall argue TV usage has become one aspect of the quotidian; often 'moving wallpaper', but still a significant reflection of who we are, and might be. In 1950 4.3% of homes had a TV set, 49.4% in 1956, and by 1964 (the 'golden age') 90%+.

In addition to this Graham Murdock has raised some relevant questions about the citizen's right to accessing television for information, and for experience. This is important in terms of whose experience we can encounter via conventional television viewing. A good deal has been said in recent years about whose faces and everyday life experience are typically portrayed on television in all formats; news, documentary, entertainments and fiction/ drama. I say more about this later in my essay, considering those social class, ethnicity and gender issues mentioned above. Murdock suggests that 'television' people have tended to believe that they have helped to create a 'shared culture' in the UK, much in line with post 1950s ideas about a more open and pluralistic society. But, questions of a fair and balanced representation of 'all' of civil society, the great cultural diversity of everyday life, are still being asked. Knowledge is power in many obvious ways, and the control of that knowledge, the values that influence choices about exactly what constitutes relevant knowledge about whom and what? (Murdock 1999)

This essay will explore the way television is very much a part of our everyday lives;

'Everyday life, it is argued, cannot be sustained without order – an order manifested in our various traditions, rituals, routines and taken for granted activities – in which we, paradoxically, invest so much energy, effort and so many cognitive and emotional resources.' (Silverstone 1994 p.1)

And; 'Television as entertainer and as informer: providing in its genres and its narratives stimulation and disturbance, peace and reassurance, and offering within their own order an expression and a reinforcement of the containing temporalities of the everyday.' (Silverstone 1994 p.19)

This very important issue for TV production and consumption is highlighted by John Ellis (2000), in that the very audio-visual technology of TV enables people to be a witness, to even bear witness, to unfolding domestic and world events. By the 1950s in the UK, TV was a medium that through non-fiction broadcasting, for example news and documentary, presented the viewer with a dynamic 'window on the world'. The fantastical in your living room, every day, part of our quotidian. This visual stimulation, information and communication; television as a visual medium with sound; working through the stages of awareness and understanding, even uncertainties. That daily inter-action between the private and the public domains of our lives. How important this was to become, for example in the way television has homogenised people in the UK in to a more national world view, quite literally showing people otherwise spatially isolated because of geography etcetera, what is happening in 'their' society. So, television has also encouraged us to reach out to other people and places, and certainly to aspirations to other lifestyles and expectations.

So much of everyday life is tied up with symbolic representations of the core aspects of that life; BBC and NHS logos for example. To paraphrase Anthony Cohen, just because someone lives in a particular place, within certain boundaries and apparently a member of some culture group does not mean that they put the same meanings on place and social life. TV is rich in symbolic representations of culture and community, but we need to acknowledge that this is a mental as well as a material based construct. (Cohen 1985)

The growth of television in the 1950s, and increasing access to it, did change family life, and fits closely with what sociologists refer to as the 'privatisation' of the family. Essentially this means that for a wide range of reasons, including re-housing, families looked inward to each other, (and huddled around the single TV set that they had, and usually rented), and while having gained access to this 'window on the world' increasingly looked outward. This issue fits closely with what I say below about the way post 1945 UK life changed. The advent of television did therefore both liberate and domesticate family life, but with variations within those families depending on class, culture group, gender and age.

As I discuss further below, TV has the capacity to impart ideas and images that become part of the stock of 'common knowledge' held by people in general. (Gripsrud 1999) And, John Ellis compliments this key idea on the significance of television in our everyday lives by arguing that;

'…television itself to a large degree, (provides) far too much information and far too little explanation. Television does not provide any overall explanation; nor does it necessarily ignore or trivialize. Television itself, just like its soap operas, comes to no conclusions. Its process of working-through (issues) is more complex and inconclusive than that.' (Ellis 1999 p.55)

This 'working-through' aspect of television drama is crucial to the manner in which what is offered to the audience in the narrative development of the

8

story in series and serial formats, gives time for issues to be resolved, or at least chewed over, talked about, assessed with regard to 'real' life. Never completely resolved in total, but often so in specific character and plot detail. I say more about this later with regard to specific examples, including key issues around just how well we are, as individuals, and/or cultural groups, prepared to deal with all this? Making sense of ourselves as well as making sense of what we encounter via television on a daily basis.

Writing in 2007, Robin Nelson makes the valid point that TV output and range is very different from 'the golden age' of the 1960s/70s. The newer technologies of transmission beyond the long-standing terrestrial channels have opened up greater possibilities for watching, including the fact that more people are prepared to pay more, separately from the cost of their TV license, to watch specific programmes. He emphasises the growth in transnational companies, especially USA ones, who with their bigger budgets and greater reach came to dominate production. The BBC increasingly moved in to this market, for example making lavish costume dramas, one off plays and serials, with an eye on the American and global market. After the mid-1950s the BBC struggled to hold the moral high-ground because their monopoly had been broken, particularly so in the field of TV drama, and pop music. Ironically perhaps this requirement of the BBC to be more populist in its productions did open more opportunities for the radical drama element to access the money and the schedules. Of course the BBC management still did their best to operate internal censorship.

In his book cited above, Alan Sinfield reminds us of some of the reasons why the 1960s has been seen as a 'golden age' for TV in general, as well as TV drama in particular. He argues that by 1970 TV had reached its liberal/radical highpoint. It should be remembered that Hugh Carleton Greene was Director General of the BBC from 1960 to 1969 and oversaw many significant innovations, even if they were mainly well within the confines of the liberal elite. The disappointments of the Wilson Labour governments of the 1964-70 period did push many of signed up members of left-culturalism

9

to abandon hopes of the BBC and ITV making more radical changes to public service broadcasting.

The pro-public sector Pilkington report on Broadcasting (with Richard Hoggart as a member) was published in 1962, and led to the opening of BBC2 in 1964. David Attenborough was the second Controller of the channel from 1965 to 1969.

Sinfield, with others cited in this essay, emphasises the sway that the left/liberal culture cohort held over the arts in the late 1950s and 1960s. Public sector TV is just one example. Public sector money and initiative led to fifteen new theatres were built across the UK between 1958 and 1970. These investments in the 'arts' were a key aspect of the determining what was 'good culture'. As I discuss in this essay how far this adequately reflected and represented the multi-cultural and diverse population and arts scene was another matter. Even in this 'golden age' there was a dominance of the 'white boys club', and the virtual invisibility of everyone else. Pilkington was of course followed by the Annan Report in 1977, which led to the creation of Channel 4, another decent proposal for public service broadcasting, which has gone so badly wrong I cannot bring myself to discuss it.

Along with the other major terrestrial broadcasters the BBC was effected by the 1990 Broadcasting Act, that required them to cede 25% of the overall production schedule to independents. This raised the possibility that these independent companies would have more editorial control of the nature of TV drama.

Nelson also cites the focus on a multicultural/ethnicities approach in terms of access to and choices to watch a wide range of culturally specific TV drama. The politics of identity is clearly a key issue here, and he does cite the usual postmodern view that there are no/fewer fixed values and criteria to guide an assessment of who interprets what in their own way. But even if 'social class' may seem to have been replaced by a more diverse identity politics linked to gender, ethnicity and age, the growth in the haves/have-nots in the UK is still a key factor in production for, and reception by, TV audiences. Class politics may have been written off by those with a vested interest in asserting that these 'traditional' social relations are not significant enough to represent these issues in TV drama, but they will not go away.

So, initially I want to discuss the emergence of TV within a UK society both recovering from World War 2, and setting out with a post-war political settlement that included the development of a 'welfare state' to replace a wartime one. After discussing these key contexts, I will then turn more specifically to a discussion about Tragedy as a dramatic form, and consider some examples.

In his 2000 book 'Television Drama', John Caughie tackles the tricky subject of 'serious drama'. He emphasises that what constitutes 'serious drama', the criteria against any drama was tested, give the 'serious test', was a task for liberal, literary middle class people. Certain works entered the canon on the say-so of people who knew best. There was a time when ITVs contribution to the serious side of Christmas scheduling was to fill Boxing Day afternoon with a Grand Opera, which I am sure they assumed no one would tune in to!

11

What do I mean by Popular Culture

Also at this early stage of my introduction I need to consider what is meant by 'popular culture'. It is widely agreed by culture theorists that popular culture means the everyday creative outcomes of the people, even in the ordinary mass-ness of the population. It is commonplace amongst specific culture groups, ways of life, symbolic forms like language, music and so on. It is the quotidian, culture is ordinary. Even a folk culture. Of, and for, the people; but which people? Also, the aesthetic boundaries between different culture groups are porous, and as I argue in this essay there are many 'outside' cultural influences that find their way in to the consciousness of people. Watching TV is one clear way in which despite our cultural specificities, we do share a great deal. TV is clearly one example of popular culture because so many people share this product of the so called creative industries. We have been extensively homogenised by these encounters with the media. However, it is important here to emphasise that different people with diverse cultural backgrounds, life experiences and personality variations, will come to, and consume TV in their own way. Individuals are essentially composed of three major ingredients; what culture group they are socialised in to, the effect on them of wider social influences, like community, schooling and work, and their own specific biography. No one else has lived our life. Given all the dimensions to our development, and the roles we take on and inhabit, we are all multiple selves. One thing we all have to do is understand the inter-relation between all these aspects of our self, and make sense of, and manage, this totality.

But watching TV is an interactive process, and Nick Stevenson argues that being so engaged with a medium like TV the individual places her/himself in a process which contributes to the moral evolution of the ego. (Stevenson 1997)

In his reflections upon the influences that took him in to drama Kenneth

12

Branagh says that watching TV drama 'went to the heart and soul of things', 'deeper than just a good story'; in his youth 'TV drama was flying!'.

So in this essay I am making a case for the value to us as human and social beings of watching serious drama, and especially perhaps, tragedy.

But, and this is a big but, the audiences for TV, and TV drama, are many and varied. You do not need a sociologist to tell you this, because we are all aware of how social class, regionality, locality, gender, ethnicity, and so on, makes for variety. Of course most of us have commonalities with others, like us, near and far.

TV and our everyday lives

As argued above we are all the outcomes of the social structures of which we are a part, that have a bearing on our lives; family, schooling, education, working life, income, and so on, secondly the culture group in to which we were born, and the culture groups we later choose to be a member of, and then our own very specific biography. No one else has led, is leading, our life! We are constantly making, and re-making, our life. This is a dynamic process. In our use of television, we make choices of what to watch, and these choices we make, can create our voice, our agency; inevitably reflecting on who 'we' are at any one time. Our values and tastes have been influenced by our everyday life encounters, our socialisation, but we are always engaged in this creation of self. How then do we fit in to ideas about the audience for television? This key question is explored in this essay.

There has been a considerable amount of research done on 'the audience' for TV, and some of this evidence is discussed in this essay. If the reader would like much more detail on this issue I would point them to Roger Silverstone's 1994 book 'Television and everyday life'.

Consumer oriented capitalism has also made inroads in to the continued existence of our separate cultural identities. Alternative cultures to the elites of society, the rich and powerful minority, have out of necessity been absorbed by the everyday workings of capitalism, which must by definition find ways to make money, to consume labour and make profits for the few. Capitalism has been very creative in drawing us in to its spending 'web', finding ways to create wants that must be satisfied if we are to enjoy a lifestyle that both reinforces and replenishes our sense of self, our identity.

Only in recent times do we now see many people of colour in TV adverts. Black lives do matter to the extent of joining the rest of us mirrored in the lifestyle promotion essential to big money making, all swimming together in the sea of a politics of selfishness, and the seeking of a possessive individualism. At last we are all identified as equally exploitable. Hurrah!

Bound up in all of this is 'object theory', a key aspect of the work of psychoanalyst Donald Winnicott, and his contemporaries in the Independent faction of post 1945 British Psychoanalytic movement. Winnicott, like John Bowlby, was very influential in child and parenting policy in the new 'Welfare State'. Put very briefly 'object theory' suggests that as we develop from infancy, we increasingly transfer our attachment away from the mother's breast to other objects (see Kohon). The having and the holding of these desired and pleasurable objects helps to maintain our mental health, and therefore the growth of an economy based on us desiring and accumulating objects has been at the centre of our lives, our sense of self, our identity. The overwhelming number of us, even within our more specific culture groups, have been exposed to and exploited by the apparently irresistible attraction of consuming objects. We have all seen the new shiny, high status lifestyle on television, this has led to a transfer of our commitment to consume beyond needs to embrace wants. Television, especially so since the arrival of commercial channels in the mid-1950s, has been the culture of choice.

In his discussion of 'everyday life' Henri Lefebvre also highlighted the role of 'objects' in the development of consumer oriented possessive individualism. He argued that due to their high status there were 'leading objects', and the car was a prime example. But where are all these cars produced, and at what 'real' cost? Vance Packard asks these questions in relation to the USA in his 1960 book 'The Waste Makers', starting with the dedication in this book;

'To my Mother and Father who have never confused the possession of goods with the good life'

Many Sociologists in the USA in the 1960s echoed these concerns with the increasing role of a consumption oriented, and advertising led production ethos; for example, David Riesman asking 'Abundance for what?'. They saw that in the USA, as elsewhere, a top down de facto cultural policy was taking

15

a stranglehold on the popular imagination.

Culture policy has always been an area of conflict, sites of struggle, and the immediate post 1945 period was no different with the social and cultural elite attempting to hold the aesthetic and moral high-ground via the arts. Increasingly the growth of the commercial influence on the arts was to undermine this control;

'The loss of aesthetic authority by an elite which was once proud of its convictions and taste is emblematic of a wider decline in deference and authority' (Mulgan 1996 p.209)

After the war the rebuilding of British society was led by the creation of the so-called 'welfare state', which for the ideologically dominant social democrats in the Establishment, meant more than just care, benefits, and services. They saw 'the arts' as 'existence goods', essential for enhancing the spiritual dimension of people's lives, and in many ways an antidote to the consequences (even then) of living in a de-industrialising capitalist society, to be increasingly dominated by the market place. Okay, by the 1980s a good deal of the traditional public = good, and commercial = bad dichotomy had waned in the artist's consciousness, due mainly to the increasing dominance of the market place realities of everyday life.

The 'great and the good', led by key people like John Maynard Keynes (who was the inspiration behind, and first chairman of, The Arts Council in 1946) did believe that high culture would trickle-down to the great unwashed over time. All that 'Sceptred Isle' stuff. In general terms the advent of 'cultural arts' policy, that the creation of the Arts Council signified, would open up conflicts with the dominant policy focus on preservation and heritage. These tensions existed until 1997, when Blair & co. shifted the balance much more towards Cultural policy, with for example, the creation of the Department of Culture, Media and Sport.

However, the stranglehold on deciding what was important, and crucially who should be exposed to it, was not broken until the late 1950s and 1960s, with the rapid growth of a commercial role in 'the arts'. One of the contradictions of this time was that this period was also dubbed the 'golden age' of TV drama. I shall return to Caughie later to explore this crucial period of production and consumption.

On the one hand there is a growing number of writers, producers and directors, who did look to public sector subsidy to develop their work, and gain access to a wider public. On the other hand, top-down controls over subsidy and production did change by the late 1960s;

'...in culture more than anywhere else, the social democratic rhetoric was in time unravelled, as it transpired that public service was for the public, not of the public, for professionals not amateurs or volunteers and for balance and sobriety, not pleasure and risk.' (Mulgan 1996 p.213)

Given these historical tensions in who could do what for whom, I do want to reiterate that the contemporary, the here and now, TV could do more to highlight these endemic contradictions in society.

Tragedy in our everyday lives

The use of tragedy, as one form of TV drama, emphasises, even exposes for all to see, a fundamental paradox in our lives, namely the raising of hope only (even knowingly) for that hope to be dashed. This possibility always was, and still is, played out against a very complex and often contradictory set of social and cultural factors which I shall explore in this essay. It is these constant tensions that determine the conditions of practice for all of those involved in TV drama.

Within the development of Modern society in the last two hundred years or so has been a constant theme of progress; philosophically, industrially, economically, politically and socially. The prospect of the creation of super-abundance, democracy, an egalitarian life, social justice, and individual freedom of choice has been promoted. Most people in the highly mechanised, capitalised and individualised society like ours have signed up for all the benefits on offer from an increasingly globalised world wide web of goodies. We have all from childhood onwards been persuaded by an increasing politics of selfishness allied to a 24/7 barrage of lifestyle advertising, a cultural domination (hegemony) that has created one paradox after another.

As Rita Felski argues;

'…only with freedom does the tragic gulf between desire and realization become possible. While this freedom may be far from absolute, modern history extends the promise of self-actualization to an ever-widening circle of persons, thereby multiplying the opportunities for human agency, miscalculation, and error, while simultaneously underscoring the painful schism between incandescent dreams and insurmountable social circumstance.' (Felski 2008 p.9)

We are all offered everything on the menu, we see it, we are told it is

18

true; the American Dream, the classless Affluent Society, opportunity, self-actualisation, freedom and so on, only for most people to actually be denied access to all this by a range of self-seeking and privileged 'gatekeepers'. Self-doubt, and a 'tail trapped in the door' lack of confidence sets in. The aspirations still exist on paper, they are regularly promoted, many (young) people even pay upfront for access to all these life enhancing goodies, only to become frustrated, disappointed, and guilty about their personal failure and so on. A wretchedness of spirit, disenchantment, sets in where a hopeful optimism had been fostered, bundled up in the many promises of unlimited opportunity for a better, more self-satisfying life. Possessive individualism at a price, including the growth of values bolstering the on-going politics of selfishness.

In response to this situation dramatists like Brecht, on the left of the political spectrum, sought to literally 'upset' the audience by deliberately seeking to alienate and discomfort them. This could emphasise the cathartic effects of fear and pity.

Given the nature of our kind of society since the 1950s, the rapid changes to technologies and so on, on the one hand, with continuity always apparent in daily life, we have seen more social and cultural conjuncture, a combination of circumstances often causing a crisis. Even by the late 1950s those who were paying attention could see the immediate, but also long-term consequences of the de-industrialisation of the UK. Progress, yes perhaps, but as I would say to my social policy students, 'not everyone experienced the swinging 60s'.

The condition of popular culture in the 1950s was also under close scrutiny, with Richard Hoggart in his 1957 book 'The Uses of Literacy' leading the way with an argument about the overwhelming of indigenous working class cultures by a brash 'colonising' pop culture from the USA. This would be felt individually and collectively. The sub-title of Hoggart's book was 'Aspects of working-class life with special reference to publications and entertainments.' (TV was in its infancy), emphasises the way in which the in-coming cultural values took ordinary people away from what they knew and did, in to a very open-ended and aspirational set of promises. Hoggart was, however, optimistic about the value of increasing access to good quality schooling and education. As Raymond Williams argued, this educational, and potentially democratising process was a 'long revolution'. For both these writers, the apparent socio-economic 'progress' of the post-war years could not hide the realities and continuing effects of significant social class differences.

This approach emphasises the idea that culture groups do have distinctive elements to their everyday lives, their culture is of, and essentially, for them, it serves their needs and reflects their interests. These cultural traits have a history, which reflect the values of that culture group, what they believe to be important and functional to reflect their life and aspirations. Forms of culture as discussed by Hoggart and others, is a form of lubrication for the known functioning of everyday life. As I discuss in this essay there was, and still is, a tendency for the producers of leisure/entertainment cultures especially to 'colonise' existing cultural forms, for example music, reproducing and re-shaping, and selling this back to people, and making money in the process.

One dimension of these issues is to do with the 'moral economy' of the family, a concept mainly developed in the UK by the social historian Edward Thompson, one of our best writers on culture, in the 1960/70s. This idea suggests that the lives of families within their specific time and place culture group have a set of understandings and values that affect their expectations of who does what for whom, and what natural, traditional rights people have. Whatever is happening within the wider economy of work and everyday life is contextualised by this moral order of what is right and proper, the due respect that is given to people regardless of their rank and role. The increased commercialisation and money dominated life of post 1945 life exposed people to these tensions, to these compromises that they were being expected to adopt. Things changed, were forced on people without any discussion, that were seen as immoral, illegitimate, and even illegal acts. Just not acceptable, and crossing a line that created outrage in people who through no fault of their own were caught up in sets of circumstances that undermined their ability to cope. This all emphasises the point that everyday cultural life is often about survival and resistance.

One aspect of these social and economic changes that impacted everyday culture was the increasing reliance on the global market place for meeting daily needs. The recovery of the post 1945 capitalist economy led to a significant consumer oriented goods and services market place. So, cultural artefacts, like TV, were created for the people. Once 'makers' of these cultural products discovered what captivated people they could shape, reinforce, and repeat what was to be consumed.

At this point some readers may wish to 'fast-forward' and read the section 'Definitions and the nature of Tragedy' (page 47 onwards) before returning to my discussion of Cultural policy, and the nature and development of TV and its uses. Otherwise stay here, fasten your belts, you are in for a culturally bumpy ride!

Cultural policy; practice and power

By the mid-1960s increasing numbers of working families buoyed by higher incomes, often as a consequence of more wives/mothers working, looked to their aspirational values being providing by the market place, and less so by the local and national State apparatus. Of course there were still many working families for whom the 'social wage'; the term conventionally given to the monetary value of care, benefits and services; was still essential for an improved quality of life. But, personal consumption in the growing marketplace did expand rapidly resulting in a set of values linked to possessive individualism rather than traditional cultural supports. (Hall 1988)

New forms of popular culture, including advertising, increasingly carried by TV, expanded alongside growth in the marketplace. One of the bitter ironies of this rush to the market, the exponential growth in the demand for goods, was the calculated choice by corporations to move the manufacture of many goods to the 'Third World', where labour costs were much lower. The 'popular culture' of strong trade unions, this collective control mechanism, pushed up wages; eventually jobs would be lost, while profits were maintained. This is an issue that keeps being addressed in this essay.

Hoggart's book was in fact one of many contributions to the on-going, but suddenly very urgent, discussion about the nature and effects of Popular Culture, i.e. all the new-ish, and rapidly expanding 'mass media of communications'. Liberal minded members of the Educational establishment were very anxious about the way in which the values that they held true were being undermined, seen as irrelevant, and replaced in the common consciousness by the widespread consumption of this new ephemera. As I say later, the politicians of the 1950s and early 1960s felt impelled to find out what on earth was going on, and respond accordingly through regulation and social controls. Popular Culture was a problem! An expanding, more socially and politically aware TV began to incorporate the radical trends

22

happening in the theatre. And, while much small scale, and niche theatre could be ignored, what appeared on TV screens could not. Ironically, the lack of choice for TV watchers in the 50s and 60s meant their increasing exposure to 'new' drama.

As TV consumers, we all take actions, but not necessarily in conditions of our own choosing. And while many people did sign up for the bright new consumer culture, and saw this as a positive move towards a less class bound society, a 're-making' of social status and opportunity, not everyone did, or could, share this new freedom. Some of the best examples of popular culture in the late 1950s and 1960s brought this paradox to our attention.

But, the rise in so called identity politics is evident here, what Raymond Williams referred to as a militant particularism, allied to the growth of possessive individualism I discuss in this essay. This has certainly had an impact on the appeal, or lack of, a socialist politics that foregrounds the collective over the individual. The Labour Party has consistently struggled with this phenomenon!

Arthur Miller discussed this line of argument in his 1949 article for The New York Times in 1949;

'Tragedy enlightens – and it must, in that it points the heroic finger at the enemy of man's freedom. The thrust for freedom is the quality in tragedy which exalts. The revolutionary questioning of the stable environment is what terrifies. In no way is the common man debarred from such thoughts or such actions.' (Quoted in Dukore 1974)

Miller went on to emphasise the crucial role of the 'writer' in that the creative impulse must understand and assert the consequences of cause and effect. The character of the hero, woman or man, drives them forward to seek their goal, their humanity regardless of the apparently impossible odds. The death of the king, or the death of a salesman?

23

The importance of a dialectical approach is also essential here because the conflicting arguments confronting the heroic person must be changed by historical events in to a synthesis, an outcome, for good or for ill. Tensions must be resolved, the story line completed, within the timeframe of the production and the scheduling. This destiny is essential to the action in whatever form that is creatively portrayed.

The combination of having something serious to say, and the articulation to say it, reminds me of C.Wright Mills, the sociologist, and contemporary of Miller, emphasising the writer's 'vocabulary of motives'.

In his book 'Modern Tragedy' Raymond Williams emphasised the importance of this historical dimension;

'My central argument…was on the deep relations between the actual forms of our history and the tragic forms within which these are perceived, articulated and reshaped.

What I …note is a strengthening of one of these forms, which in cultures like my own has become temporarily dominant and indeed, at times, overwhelming.

In its most general sense this can be expressed, simply, as a widespread loss of the future.' (Williams 1979 p.207/8)

Williams sought to emphasise the connected meanings in our lives, which can be revealed through dramatic representation. Tragedy can be seen to expose for our examination the continuous sense of life, but by no means taking place in a neat straight line.

Williams is here discussing what I have mentioned above, that the reliance by people on the continuance of a liberal democratic society fuelled by the post 1945 social democratic ideology, the 'post-war' settlement of a state led collective context to everyday life. This orthodox world view of thirty years standing, was however, too shallowly planted in to the political soil of social and economic life, and, by the late 1970s, all too easily swept away by the rise of a hard-nosed money led neo-liberalism. The State had shaped and managed this progressive infrastructure, assuring 'the people' that they would continue to be looked after, but, the people were not sufficiently in control of this destiny.

I added my own reflection on this situation in 2008;

'As I write this, there is a good deal of discussion as to whether democracy is in decline in Britain, and if indeed there is a democratic deficit in our lives. Moreover, what is actually being mourned is not democracy, because we have never had it, but the loss of that hope we had in achieving a democratic life.' (Astley 2008 p.7/8)

Writing in 1961, Raymond Williams acknowledged the complexity of any analysis of our diverse everyday cultural life;

'We need to distinguish three levels of culture, even in its most general definition. There is the lived culture of a particular time and place, only fully accessible to those living in that time and place. There is the recorded culture, of every kind, from art to the most everyday facts: the culture of a period. There is also, as the factor connecting lived culture and period cultures, the culture of the selective tradition.' (Williams 1961 in Bennett p.49)

Throughout this essay I will be discussing these issues associated with Popular Culture, and will emphasise again that definitions do vary a good deal, but crucially Williams himself always insisted that 'culture is ordinary' i.e. an everyday and shared culture. But whose culture we are discussing, even celebrating, remains a key issue. (This approach was reinforced by Paul Willis in his 1970 book 'Common Culture'). As Williams argued TV watching has a 'flow', one programme after another, with usually no logical reason for this, but all watched! I recall watching the surreal final episode of Alan Bleasdale's 'Boys from the Blackstuff', which was immediately followed by live football from Liverpool.

Williams talked about 'culture' as a whole way of life, and tackled the complex issue of each person's agency; power to affect change in their own, and other's lives; and the social and economic 'structures'; community, family, schooling, the workplace, exerted controls over everyday life. Williams' concept 'structures of feeling' sought to describe the collective, community based, sentiments and values that came as a result of both agency and structure.

In many ways the generation of dramatists that sought to transform the genre in the 1950s/60s where part of a structure of feeling, a commitment to a new medium, a politically unstable period, and a commitment to a radical intervention. I will say more about this later.

The third of Williams' levels above is what I am emphasising as the way in which 'artists' tell us stories about our pasts, present, and possible futures, even utopian ones. And, of course, as Williams argues, this is selective, the cultural canon, the conventional. The point is who makes this selection, and for what purpose?

But before we get to a discussion of what cultural practice can do, might do, we need to reinforce the point that most 'art' is still elitist in both the ideas that exist conventionally about what it is, and also who it is for. Paul Willis in his book cited above says;

'The institutions and practices, genres and terms of high art are currently categories of exclusion more than inclusion. They have no real connection with most young people or their lives. They may encourage some artistic specializations but they certainly discourage much wider and more general symbolic creativity... If some things count as "art", the rest must be "non-art". Because "art" is in the "art gallery", it can't therefore be anywhere else. It is that which is special and heightened, and not ordinary and everyday.' (Willis 1990 in Gray p.206)

Also in Gray's book (1993), Nicholas Garnham reinforces what I argue in this essay about the nature and role of the culture industries. My discussion below, of Ideological Cultural Apparatuses (ICAs) shares with Garnham the insistence that these 'arts industries' are essentially the same as any other industrial entity in contemporary society. One major difference is of course the economics of the everyday existence for arts organisations; galleries, theatres, performing companies, the BBC and so on. The role of subsidy has conventionally and contemporaneously relied on State subsidy in addition to other forms of income like Lottery money and sponsorship. And, the influence of the commercial sector in the everyday lives of people in 'the arts', individuals and organisations, was ever present. By the 1980s a whole generation of creative people had accustomed themselves to this reality.

The significance of the National Lottery for culture and cultural change cannot be ignored. John Major created this institution in 1993, which fed in to the 'get rich quick' fantasies of ordinary working people while funding the arts, a wonderful swindle dressed up as a way of subsidy. After 1979 Thatcher, and her associates, set about changing both the economic base of the UK, and the prevailing culture. The Labour government under Callaghan had emptied out the last remnants of the post 1945 prevalence of the social democratic ideology of collectivism. Thatcher & co. set about the task of changing the political narrative to one of individualism and free choice in the market place. The playwright, David Edgar said;

'...this deft sleight of hand is reflected in the actual processes of change: the brilliance of Thatcher is not...in its economics but rather in its politics, or, even ratherer, in its capacity to pursue political ends by fiscal means, to express essentially social objectives in political language, to achieve economic goals by way of a transformation of culture.' (Edgar 1988 p.13)

27

Edgar is discussing political dominance through a changed culture. The so-called neo-liberals, Thatcher, and up to and including Blair and Brown after 1997, had to find a way to steer the national conversation away from the dominance of the State in matters of funding, to one where these matters of subsidy would be left to the Market. Even when the Blair/Brown government did insist on the need for increased funding of the arts, the actual money was subjected to a cost/benefit set of rules.

Edgar's 1988 argument was shared by Robert Hewison in 2014;

'There is a popular prejudice that politics and the arts should not have too much to do with each other; yet they have important things in common. They are both ways of making meaning. They are concerned with values, engage the emotions, and try to change minds.' (Hewison 2014 p.3)

Blair put the arts, the 'creative industries', at the centre of his extension of the Thatcherite pre-eminence of the Market to provide all;

'Creative Britain needed a creative economy in order to ensure the continuous innovation on which growth depended. This would be served by a "creative class" whose occupation was the production of signs and symbols that could be consumed in commodified form.' (Hewison 2014 p.5)

Cultural policy became an essential part of economic policy for regeneration. The message to the creative arts was clear, we can arrange for you to have the money you need, but, only by our rules! No surprises then that the title of Hewison's book is 'Cultural Capital'.

Indeed, the issues about 'culture' and money that Hewison raises, emphasises the importance of the 'creative industries' to successive governments. As I discuss elsewhere in this essay, the whole idea of seeing the work and output of 'creatives' in society as the best big economic opportunity, and money making scheme, hopefully filling the gap left from the decline of manufacturing, has

28

many critics. The degradation of 'the arts' as a consequence of being shackled to a commercial sector take-over has never worn well with a significant section of the liberal-artistically inclined population.

Blair and Brown most certainly embraced the advent of 'Cool Britannia' from the Thatcher years, and 'talked-up' a new creative Britain under the auspices of New Labour after 1997. However, the 'culture vultures' as described by Elliott and Atkinson in their 2007 book 'Fantasy Island', were prone to exaggerate the size and economic significance of the 'creative industries';

'A large number of people work in the creative industries, broadly defined, although not nearly as many as the hype would suggest. There are three times as many people working in domestic service as there are in advertising, television, video games, film, the music business and design combined; the creative industries represent around one in 20 of the people working in Britain today. Between them they account for around 4 per cent of all UK exports of goods and services...it is hard to make serious money.' (Elliott and Atkinson 2007 p.88)

On the arts funding issue since the much enthused about extra money for the arts by Blair and Brown, it is true that in recent years there has been an attempt to spread funding more generally across community based arts activity, and the various forms of the Arts Council are making limited inroads in to the considerable imbalance between the 'big-hitters' of the arts world, and everyone else seeking subsidy. Garnham also reminds us that all of this money finding its way to worthy recipients seeks to embrace the unique important of 'the artist' as distinct from the grass-roots practitioner or audience.

It is also true that organisations like the Gulbenkian Foundation have encouraged liberal minded managers of arts institutions, like galleries for example, to find more innovative ways for members of the public; arty or otherwise; to gain access to the substantial resources held in trust by these institutions. Because most people, even those who do occasionally enter an art gallery, or attend the subsidised theatre, those special kinds of people who should have an entitlement to this often public money being used for private purposes, do not see themselves as 'artists'. Identity is most certainly an issue here, whether top-down or bottom-up.

I have argued that identity formation is consistently a struggle against conformity, and cultural diversity in the UK, as elsewhere, is a key issue here;

'For several at Open University summer school, I had the pleasure of giving a regularly updated talk on 'Six Propositions about Culture and Identity'. These six were;

1. It is to be welcomed the the UK is a more multi-cultural society (when there are continuity as well as change issues).
2. Human action creates culture, contributing to the personal and social expressions of identity.
3. Culture reflects the diversity and semi-autonomy of "us"…
4. But, there are contradictions and conflicts which arise. People's aspirations versus forces of control; struggles occur, often located in particular sites.
5. However, people invariably feel that their needs can only be met by engaging in these struggles.
6. Culture as articulated opposition to exclusion, and these marginal cultures as an antidote to alienation and oppression.'
    (Astley 2008 p.14/15)

In this respect mention should be made of the work of Stuart Hall, and his idea about 'sites of struggle' in everyday culture which I have alluded to above. These 'struggles' occur because of the downward pressure of routine and domesticating popular 'entertainment', is met by a demand by individuals and groups that everyday cultural and creative practice should be challenging this patronising and controlling situation. However, as I discuss in this essay, the wish to use creative culture to resist the power of elite decision makers and creators, and demand liberation, is all very well, but is a long term freedom for all actually achieved? I raised this issue in my study of The Beatles. Apparently 'All you need is love' was not enough? (Astley 2006).

Can contemporary TV help us with issues of morality and spirituality?

Henri Lefebvre the French sociologist, writing in the 1950s, devoted a good deal of his analysis to uncovering the 'hidden' desires, dreams, frustrations and hopes of people within their everyday lives along the lines I have argued here. He was adamant that one essential way for people to liberate themselves from the overwhelming, and overbearing, daily routine was through creativity, seeking out and using whatever artistic means came to hand. Structures of feeling manifested themselves in both an aesthetic disposition, often associated with popular/folk cultures, and the developing of techniques to express those feelings that then nourished the possibility of a better future. (Lefebvre 1968)

And, talk of 'hidden desires' reminds me of Karl Mannheim, writing thirty years before in 'Ideology and Utopia', who wrote about the survival of western 'civilization', propped up by the European version of 'the American Dream' with a combination of regular top-down fictions, the ideologies, and the wish-dreams that are the utopias that give people (false) hope. A phenomenon that orthodox Marxists have called false consciousness.

A major aspect of my interest in emphasising just how vital popular culture is to our personal and collective understanding of life has to do with our reliance on the State to care for us, to be the facilitating context to our on-going stability, to avoid a precarious existence, and to alleviate uncertainty, even pain. While many of those actively running the State apparatus in many forms, including crucially schooling and other aspects of education, have continued to do their thing, they have in fact been superseded in the dissemination of ideas by the influence of popular cultures. Many years ago I developed the concept of Ideological Cultural Apparatuses (ICAs), mentioned above; (including the media in all its forms including popular cultures) to emphasise this very significant change in society and everyday life. People's everyday gaze, and their quest for contemporary information and advice, had been diverted away from what the State was conventionally offering, 'enlightenment' was to be found elsewhere. Even basic information that we 'need' to lead our lives has increasing come from the media in one form or another. It is quite clear that what most people say they know about health care, or how policing works, is derived from fictional; or at least 'factional', sources. If you want to know how this or that product is produced, watch a TV series; however, these programmes are not documentaries, they are entertainment, and headed up by a 'TV person', a 'Jack/Jill of all trades', or a celebrity, who almost certainly derived that status from being on TV. TV, like so much other media offers us a simulacrum, a simulation of real life which has been created and packaged for a particular programming slot in the conventional schedules. It worked last time, the sponsors were happy, so do it again.

It is also important here to emphasise the 'gaze' and 'watch' aspect of the above. Starting with Marshall McLuhan in the 1960s, (The Medium is the Message!) and certainly contributed to by Raymond Williams in the 1970s, theorists have argued that television is a different medium, a visual kaleidoscope offering visual stimulation in our domestic setting, that did make it special. As discussed elsewhere in this essay, the 'home' as the setting for TV watching is a key issue. And, TV is different from cinema based film in many ways, to be discussed, and crucially, who watches TV in the dark? The 'space' aspect of watching TV is also relevant, as, for example, we have moved from the whole family watching one TV set, to many families having multiple monitors in the household. Also we know that many of those monitors will not be carrying 'conventional' TV programmes. As TV screens became larger writers and directors could use that extra dimension, more close-ups, and more outside broadcasting scenes, to make a dramatic or continuity/context point. Close-ups have always been a key stimulation effect of the cinema screen, and since the marvellous advent of the live screening of theatrical productions directly, and in real time from theatres to the cinema screen has brought the viewer much closer to the action; theatre in-the-round with a difference. As discussed elsewhere in this essay the inter-relation between writers, producers, directors and actors has shifted;

'Up to the end of the nineteenth century the actor dominated the theatre, playwrights being generally required to provide situations in which he could be seen at his best. With the advent of Ibsen and his followers, however, the text became all-important, and actors had to adapt themselves to the new conditions. Realistic dialogue, in conversational style, took the place of rhetoric and declamation; gestures became more constrained, the scenery presented an accurate representation of the place and period of the play. The illusion of reality was greatly helped by the almost universal adoption of the box-set.' (Hartnoll 1968 p.240)

The now conventional 'box-set' of the theatre stage, has been replicated by the relatively small scale TV screen, set amongst domestic detritus as already discussed.

The setting and role of the audience

The family home is often the centre of domestic melodrama, and a great deal has been made of this in drama, TV based and otherwise. It is not surprising therefore that many of the writers of TV drama have wanted to avoid this convention, and focusing on tragedy is an option.

I should also acknowledge that 'the family' and the internal, often 'political' dynamics of family life, are consistently used as a dramatic device to pursue other issues, for example class politics and struggle for change. It is clear that writers can also start out with a family set drama because the audience lives with this dominant and conventional social institution, and people think they know about family! The writer can, however, smuggle in a parallel narrative to address their other motives for the drama.

We also should acknowledge the experimentation that came with growth of TV in the late 1950s.

Reconsidering the 'Golden Age' of TV drama

A growing number of creative and technically able producers, in the widest sense, adopted an experimental approach to the uniqueness of TV. One such focus came with the creation in 1959 of the Langham Group of BBC drama producers and directors. Basically they believed that the special nature of TV, as a visual medium, required a new way of doing drama; visualisation. The content also needed to follow this experimental road of social realism, with for example using TV cameras to create a 3D effect on the small screen. In deed some members of that Group argued that these production values were more important than writers. Not a view shared by most creative people involved in TV drama! Anthony Pelissier, a former theatre and film director was a leading activist in the Langham Group, keen to exploit the technical possibilities of the medium for poetry, dance and story-telling. The Group produced three plays, to mixed reviews, but, the quest for a new social realist drama to exploit the unique qualities of TV developed rapidly with the BBC, and ITV companies like Granada. To emphasise the domestic context of TV drama ABC launched 'Armchair Theatre' which attracted many of the best writers and production staff of the day, and unheard of audiences. ABC produced 'Armchair Theatre' from 1956 to 1968, and Thames TV continued the programme until 1974.

At the BBC Don Taylor produced David Mercer's plays, while in 1964 James MacTaggart and Ken Loach produced and directed the six-part series of plays 'Diary of a Young Man', written by Troy Kennedy Martin and John McGrath. Like many other plays written at this time Mercer argued, through his characters, that the post-war developments in society were consistently promoted as 'progress'. This was especially so when so many of the industries that dominated working class life had, or were, changing, along with shifting values. The drama of the late 1950s and 1960s sought to dispute that these changes added up to 'progress' for the majority of ordinary people, by giving voice to the contradictions bound up in ways of life, ideas and actions; an alternative account of the times. This drama underpinned Richard Hoggart's questioning of the interplay between 'material improvement and cultural loss', the unfolding nature of change and adaption.

The BBC also had the good fortune to employ Huw Wheldon, who amongst many other senior roles at the BBC, created and headed-up 'Monitor' from 1958 to 1964. This was experimental TV at its best, with Wheldon insisting on the fore-grounding of Imagination as the driving creative force. Ken Russell was one of film-makers inspired by Wheldon who said that 'Monitor was and still remains the one and only English experimental film school ever, and Huw Wheldon was its guiding genius.'

This explicitly experimental phase of realising, in both senses, the opportunities that the special character of TV offered, set up the 'Golden Age' of British TV drama. (For much more on this see Mulvey and Sexton)

I should also add that John McGrath set up the 7:84 theatre company in 1974, and like Joan Greenwood, developed a left-wing theatrical response to changing, but not changing, society. The 7:84 represented the 7% of British society that owned 84% of the wealth!

In his book on 'Culture' Eagleton argues along these lines in terms of the new access the growing TV audience had;

'For the first time in history, it has become possible for millions of people to listen simultaneously to a Verdi opera or watch a Chekov play. A film or television production of a Dickens or Jane Austen novel can bear fruit in hundreds of thousands of bookshop sales' (Eagleton 2016 p.145/6)

I can go to my local cinema in Devon and watch the live streaming of a production on stage in London. 'High' culture and the people who both embraced that exclusiveness, and basked in the status this affords, have now been overtaken by the totality of the Culture Industries, those ICAs, control all, and nothing. This totality looks invincible, but in fact does not completely control the creativity that goes on in the periphery of everyday life where people ignore the odds and get on with making 'art'.

Over time the amount of TV available to watch has increased exponentially, or as Bruce Springsteen put it, 'eighty-seven channels and nothing to watch.'. Rob Young in his 2021 book, 'The Magic Box: Viewing Britain through the Rectangular Window', focuses on the period from the late 1950s to the late 1980s. The late 1950s is particularly significant because the Conservative government broke the BBCs monopoly by permitting commercial TV from the mid-50s. Just as significant in recent years has been the shift from terrestrial to satellite broadcasting, down-loading, streaming and the like.

As Sukhdev Sandhu says in his Guardian review of Young's book;

'It portrays its subject as an experimental educational centre that offered an alternative national curriculum. Television in those days harboured deviants.' (Sandhu 2021)

I would add here that those who have held ownership, power and control of society's key institutions; those ICAs, have needed to constantly re-educate the population in to thinking and acting in a way that suits the interests of capital accumulation, and the maintenance of privilege.
(For a detailed discussion of the nature of power within the discussion of cultural theory see Gibson's 'Culture and Power' '2007')

The BBC charter aims are to 'educate, inform and entertain', while ITV entered in to our consciousness to 'entertain, inform and educate.'

Having opened the Pandora's Box of commercial television, the State under the auspices of Tory and Labour, was sent in to paroxysms of expensively researched panic over the effects of 'the idiot box' on children and young people.

The original broadcasters did at least nod in the direction of a modernist knowledge based approach setting; an 'improving' agenda. Broadcasting now, along with the world wide web, has moved on in a post-modern free-for-all, essentially a cornerstone of the advertising and entertainment business.

In this respect the 'ideology' in the ICAs is important here because most of popular culture; especially so in broadcasting; tends to be politically right of centre. This is not always a self-conscious 'editorial' decision to be on the right, but often a casual and myopic reinforcement of the conventional, a lazy embracing of the cultural-political status quo. The message is carried in a familiar narrative maintained by those both privileged and reluctant to change the balance of power, culturally or otherwise.

One aspect of this situation is the notion of balance in the telling of the stories, news and so on, by those editorial agents in the media. This is certainly true for the BBC, and for BBC News output in particular. There is an obsessive insistence on maintaining balance in representing the various/different sides of an argument, an issue. However, as with such 'pluralist' approaches to everyday practice, the balanced point is located someway to the political right of centre. One example to mention was the Brexit referendum debates. What the voting public saw and heard on the leave side was a motley collection of 'Little Englanders' and free trade fanatics; Farage, Johnson, Gove et al. I did not once hear the principled socialist argument for abandoning the EU bureaucracy and its commitment to global capitalism.

This thinking stands in contrast to the attempts of a minority of 'artists/ producers' to challenge this taken-for-granted-ness, and offer an alternative that raises hope for something else, a better society.

This whole situation has been reinforced, and greatly expanded by the internet, the world wide web, and so-called 'social media'. Not the least of reasons for these shifts to have happened is that those in control of the State apparatus are so out of touch with what people's everyday lives are really like they continue to offer, with their usual 'gatekeeping' approach, a 'one size fits all' solution to all manner of services. When this provision fails to work in the way they expect it to, the alleged recipients are blamed. Another of the unintended consequences of social policy and practice.

A claim is often made that popular culture, in its many forms – TV, radio, music, film, literature, fine art, internet and video based games, and so on – is often an account of real life. Realism on the screen? I acknowledge that these media also produce and carry a variety of fantasy, but even here we are usually looking at the deliberate use of allegory to tell us a story, to convey truths about the human condition.

But, this is not real life, it is an 'artistic' take on real life, on the quotidian, interpreted with meanings attached, and attributed to this situation and that. This can then be understood as real life.

Linda Nochlin, the art critic, made this point in her 1971 study, 'Realism';
'A basic cause of confusion bedevilling the notion of Realism is its ambiguous relationship to the highly problematical concept of reality.' (Nochlin 1971 p.13)

Consumers of this material culture, these 'products', then bring their own interpretation to the process. And, in a cyclical way life begins to imitate art as well as art imitating life! The pretence of reality is important. Continuity of narrative is a key feature of TV fiction, in series and serials, especially in soaps. It is clear that over many decades the viewers and listeners of dramas do believe that the situations and characters are realistic, and even real. The BBC has consistently received mail for characters in dramatic productions. This has gone well beyond Royal Mail's problem with post for Santa!

The one-off drama is different primarily because of the long term character development associated with serials and soaps. Because there are far fewer one-off dramas now, the audience is helped to associate with the commonplace schedule story and character development.

TV drama of the last fifty years has been characterised by debates and 'insider' and often theoretical arguments about dramatic styles. Considering the 'real life' issue is an example here. The 1960s era of Ken Loach and Tony Garnett's collaboration, that created 'Up the Junction' and 'Cathy Come Home' for example, opted for a documentary style of the presentation of a story; getting out of the studio with their 16mm camera. This naturalistic approach brought serious drama, to put on to the TV screen an account of a pressing social, cultural, and political issue of the day. These plays 'argued' that these issues required a response, even social reform. I watched these TV dramas, often with tragic characters as key aspects of the story, and thought about the social reform agenda of Charles Dickens, or the moral discomfort of Hardy.

This concern with defining real life also emphasises the additional problem of using the concept popular culture without suggesting that it is a homogeneous category. It is not, and the various interpretations of life's events underlines this.

It might well be that everyday life for most people is poor, precarious and without much hope of anything better? Even the prospect of heaven does ring true any longer. Creatives use the medium of Tragedy to make this point to their audiences; the bigger the better; in order to raise consciousness of the contexts of life that explains their misery, pointing not only the road of struggle and heroism, but the overwhelming necessity, and possibility, for redemption and change?

As I discuss elsewhere in this essay the criticism of melodrama has often been that dramatists provide an 'opt out' clause from the true horrors, miseries and pain of everyday life, often for example insisting on a 'happy' ending. The pleasure of the performance etcetera overcoming the reality of pain it may allude to, but essentially mask, or dilute.

41

Stuart Hall discussed the cultural complexity here;

'We understand struggle and resistance, nowadays, rather better than we do reform and transformation. Yet "transformations" are at the heart of the study of popular culture. I mean the active work on existing traditions and activities, their active re-working, so that they care in a different way: they appear to "persist", yet, from one period to another, they come to stand in a different relation to the ways working people live and the ways they define their life. Transformation is the key to the long and protracted process of the "moralisation" of the labouring classes, and the "demoralisation" of the poor, and the "re-education" of the people. Popular culture is neither, in a "pure" sense, the popular traditions of resistance to these processes, nor is it the forms which are superimposed on and over them, It is the ground on which the transformations are worked.' (Hall in Samuel 1981 p.228)

In the development of Hall's analysis of the popular arts within popular culture, he often discussed the concept of 'sites of struggle' mentioned earlier; the particular places and forms of art and culture where transformative strategies are tried out, for example breaking the conventional ways in which people's lives are represented through drama etcetera, but are resisted by those powerful gatekeepers who control the arts agenda and content. This struggle for control over what appears on our TV screens and so on, is also complicated by the acquiescence of many consumers to the conventional values and ways of seeing that dominate our everyday lives.

Hall often sought to emphasise the commonplace nature of popular art and culture;

'Popular art…is essentially a conventional art which restates, in an intense form. Values and attitudes already known; which reassures and reaffirms, but brings to this something of the surprise of art as well as the shock of recognition.' (Hall 1964 p.66)

Hall touches on an argument I have consistently made; for example, in my book on The Beatles Phenomenon (Astley 2006), that those who control the popular arts select conventional aspects of ordinary people's lives, to then turn this material in to an entertainment form to play back to that very audience, at a price! The end result, usually, is another episode of 'bread and circuses' for the masses.

And, while on the developing issue of popular arts within popular culture, I should emphasise differences, and the similarities between 'popular culture', and 'mass culture' quoting Caughie again on how these often emotive words, 'popular' and 'mass' have been used;

'When the terms are applied to culture, the etymological distinction can be read as a convenient condensation of two distinct histories. "Mass culture", within cultural studies, resonates not only with an etymology which associates the masses with fusible matter waiting inertly to be fashioned, but also with the pessimistic tradition of Adorno and the Frankfurt School (1930s/40s) which poses that inertia against the aggressive advances of the "consciousness industries". "Popular culture", in contrast, seems to have behind it a memory of the people as agents of their development, a memory which finds its focus in Britain in certain histories of popular resistance to the advance of capital in the nineteenth century, and which has often taken the form in cultural politics and cultural study of a Utopian desire to restore culture to the people and the people to their culture.' (Caughie 1986 in MacCabe p.158)

Given the heritage of this political cultural pessimism, and prevailing negative attitudes towards the 'creative industries', I have to ask myself can popular culture in its many forms, including TV drama, actually be a positive force for change. Can the over-indulged working masses of Western civilisation be encouraged and cajoled in to grasping their agency, ask difficult questions about the motives of those with power and control in the media, be a creative force for change? Are these aesthetically energised creative activists, the 'shock troops' of radical popular culture in our societies, and be the proselytizers we need to wake us from our lazy cultural slumber? Can they take on, and challenge through their creativity, the hegemony; the cultural dominance; of the ruling and controlling elites in contemporary society? Will anyone take any notice of them? As creative artists can we assert the value of popular culture as a force for new ideas and change, opposing the latest clever, arty, knowing, advertisement encouraging us to realise our freedom and salvation in buying something? A commodities route to spiritual health?

We need to ask ourselves whether public service broadcasting has a responsibility to bring an alternative perspective to our everyday lives. A special role for TV drama, even giving recent trends, a return to the single play format, the very nature of such challenges our conventions? It is clear that TV broadcasting as a cultural form has had, could have, a unique role to play. Could the 1966 TV production of 'Cathy Come Home' (which I discuss in more detail below) be replicated today? Even if it was, do we believe that it would have the same impact, be so controversial, as then?

Herbert Marcuse, with Adorno a member of the Frankfurt School, had been consistently optimistic about the revolutionary potential of working people, certainly through their creative response to both oppression and repression. However, in 1964 he published probably his most well-known book, 'One Dimensional Man', which was most definitely pessimistic about the chances of working people confining a consumer led capitalism to the dustbin of history;

'The fundamental thesis of One Dimensional Man is that the technology of advanced industrial societies has enabled them to eliminate conflict by assimilating all those who in earlier forms of social order provided their voices or forces of dissent. Technology does this partly by creating affluence. Freedom from material want...' (MacIntyre 1970 p.63)

Marcuse, along with many other radical theorists of social change was bitterly disappointed that post 1945 capitalism had not failed, or been replaced by socialist economies in the West. However, the course of political and cultural struggle continues in many forms, which is why I have to ask the question above.

Two important proselytizers, Hall and Whannel, cited above, wanted to discuss the Popular arts in a similar way as William Morris, a century earlier, needed to discuss, bring in to the spotlight, 'the decorative arts', the everyday-day-ness of ornamentation in people's lives that needed both improvement in quality and status. Convention plays a key part in what is produced and promoted at certain times. I mentioned The Beatles above whose management team took them down the cinema film road, emulating Elvis Presley of a decade before. Both manifestations used the filmic route to entertaining the masses by bringing together a few okay songs with a very thin story line. This was the way to win hearts and minds, and like Cliff Richard et al appeal to a growing and more diverse consumer base.

Responses by audiences for all these productions matter, and engagements and adaptions take place; transformations happen for good or for ill.

To paraphrase E.P.Thompson, the working classes have continued 'making' themselves through the many social and cultural interactions of everyday life, including embracing these multimedia, mass produced commodities, which were the in-thing to do. However, in many ways people still lacked agency; they did not have any significant long term control of the development of a cultural life. What was not addressed by these forms of cultural consumption was an alternative artistic life that both discusses their subordinate condition, and also impels them to transform social relations in to a better, fairer, more socially just society for all. The creative and radicalising nature of the arts offers both a motive and a means via a transformative practice, to change life.

The vast majority of working class people have indeed been shaped by social changes; industrial, economic, environmental, familial, legal and so on. But, they have also dealt with the reality of all these changes through resistance as well as by compromise and containment. Adoption and adaption, experiential and experimental. Artistic creativity has always been a key aspect of how people deal with change, and the heightened alienation that role change and displacement create. Not the least of issues here is that cultural commodities; TV, music, literature, drama and so on, are constantly changing, and must then be assessed, incorporated or denied, within the context of everyday values, and the pressures of living a life. Food comes before philosophy!

Raymond Williams in his 'Modern Tragedy', cited above, argues that the three key explanatory theories that have come to dominate the thinking of modern life are Marxism, Freudianism and Existentialism, each posing a question;

'Man can only achieve his full life only after violent conflict; man is essentially frustrated, and divided against himself, while he lives in society; man is torn by intolerable contradictions, in a condition of essential absurdity.' (Williams p.189)

On the basis of these daunting explanations of who we are, and why we are where we are, the enlightened and radical artist has no alternative other than to use any tool at her or his disposal to show this to people in general. Telling a story, an allegory even, in whatever medium to get the message across, to jolt a person, the people, out of their consumer culture stupor. In these circumstances why not use tragedy as an effective dramatic form?

Before looking at more examples and arguments about TV and drama in my section below on 'Using the tragic form…', I should offer the reader some basic definitions of Tragedy.

Definitions and the nature of Tragedy

At this point in my essay I wish to focus more specifically on the concept of Tragedy, and compliment this with some recent examples. We should acknowledge that the popular culture products of all media types on offer to us has contained a great deal of melodrama, especially so examples of the endless 'cops and robbers' genre products offered up as entertainment. This is certainly significant here as I wish to offer a critique of one such TV series as an example of Tragedy used as a focal point in the story telling. However, as often in the past, our experience of Tragedy in a vernacular form has, does and can matter, can create an opportunity to see, understand and consider the nature of the tragic in our lives. Commentators since the Greeks have emphasised the value of all sharing in the tragic experience process. As audience, through whatever medium, we can see the unfolding of tragic events, and what happens to the tragic character(s). We can and do relate all this to our own lives, the whole inter-connected fragility and precariousness of it all. We can learn from this process.

It is certainly true that Moral Philosophy has focused a good deal on the tragic nature of everyday life, and moral philosophers have consistently asked questions about our own moral life. Are we capable, able, and willing, to take responsibility for own moral state, and actions that we take. One such moral philosopher, Friedrich Nietzsche, argued that the majority of people in his time had a 'slave morality', 'the blinkers of the herd'; they were told what to think, what values to embrace, and never take personal responsibility for their own part in unfolding events in life. The tragic character can however be elevated to a higher realm of thought and action.

I have already argued in this essay that most people have embraced a consumer culture possessive individualism, 'the religion of comfortableness', and a timid mediocrity in the face of such world-wide challenges. For some this has come to mean 'the unbearable lightness of being' (Kundera), never

47

venturing beyond the 'script' of conventional everyday life to offer an educated challenge.

Being a tragic character, and being a character cast in a Tragedy, is not exclusive to the gods, or even celebrities, we can all (potentially) fill that role. These experiences with the cultural material like TV productions, could then open up a space to debate the ways to hopefully move out of these pessimistic, and pusillanimous scenarios? Take actions to avoid such situations if at all possible. There is a creative dialectic at work here for us to engage with, we may want to deny such aspects of everyday humanity, but here it is, set out for us to see and feel angry, sad and uncomfortable about. For example, many theorists of Tragedy emphasise the chaos created by tragic events, and the inter-relationship between disturbance and transcendence. An understanding of the dialectic of Tragedy here is to recognise the way in which opposed facts, feelings and emotions resolve themselves in to a condition, a realisation, beyond that. Suffering and endurance, death or redemption perhaps? Tragic drama creates anxiety, is there resolution to follow? Tragic characters have a psychology as well as a physiology. Does the drama, and the performance draw that out?

'...that representation of personal suffering and heroism which we call tragic drama is distinctive of the western tradition. It has become so much a part of our sense of the possibilities of human conduct...private anguish on a public stage.' (Steiner 1961 p.3)

It has also been argued that Tragedy conveys conflict within the person, while in melodrama conflict between persons, and popular culture in all its guises, will offer us accounts of the high and lows of everyday life;

'Comedy laughs the minor mishaps of its characters away: drama solves all the difficulties which it allows to arise; and melodrama, separating good from evil in simple lines, distributes its rewards and punishments in accordance with the principles of a naïve justice...' (Krutch p.872)

Comic drama laughs in the face of misery, an asset that I am reminded of when I listen to singer/songwriters like Leonard Cohen, Nick Cave, and even The Smiths. Even in the most dire of Shakespeare's Tragedies there is a comic turn; the gatekeeper in Macbeth, the grave scene in Hamlet, and the antics of The Fool in Lear.

Tragedy and comedy cannot adopt either way alone to deal with life's recurrent problems, and those modern dramatists who seek to expose the many fundamental issues associated with gross inequalities, and the lack of a 'voice' in a contradictory society, invariably use a synthesis of dramatic form.

'If farce shows us knaves and fools, if melodrama shows us villains and heroes, what do comedy and tragedy show us? The best brief answer, I think, is that they show us the same four characters in more complex forms.' (Bentley 1965 p.263)

So, what about definitions of tragedy, and this concepts place within the current contexts of our lives? We have been living through a very demanding period, (2020/21) dominated by the Covid-19 pandemic. There have been many tragic consequences of this public and personal health crisis. Many people have described this as a tragedy, but strictly speaking this is not so because, as already discussed, 'Tragedy' is actually the description of a dramatic form, like a play, film, novel, or opera. All of which is likely to develop empathy in us for others; we have seen this during the pandemic. Perhaps one aspect of the civilising process?

As already argued Tragedies are a form of drama based on human suffering, and usually the terrible, or sorrowful events that befall people; often the 'lonely' individual cut adrift from every day inter-actions; and frequently, their families. The tragic amidst the trivial, in the midst of life we are in death! A morbid sentiment, yes, but the daily news continually brings this to us.

Catharsis is a key aspect of Tragedy, simply put, the process of raising our emotions and feelings to a level of consciousness where we are encouraged to address these feelings by working through the highs and lows, the snakes and ladders, the laughter and tears, of what we have experienced. At the end of this journey of the unfolding of these life forming, life changing events, is there understanding, even redemption for us, making up for past injury?

Another dimension to Tragedy; and to be found in all the arts; is that of irony, the use of words, music or visual stimuli, to express a meaning other than the literal, obvious meaning. This is the incongruity between the actual circumstance and the expected or appropriate result, for example, on being let down by someone to respond with 'oh thanks very much, that's really great!'

Just think about poor Hamlet; confused, angry, uncertain about being King, life and loves; not knowing about some actions being taken by others. Hamlet is a typical example of 'the tragedy of circumstances'. Or Romeo and Juliet, who despite all the family/tribal hatred, believe that 'all you need is love'; driven by circumstances and misfortune to early deaths. Both of these scenarios have elements of miscalculation as well. These, like many others, and like the three characters in 'Unforgotten', discussed below, are tragic characters, presented to us in dramatic form to remind us all of the paradoxical nature of everyday life, even the end of hope? Tragedy also concerns itself with these moral questions, what is right and wrong; how should we lead our lives, can we be ourselves and be fair minded?

'Tragedy…entails perhaps the most direct, single-minded, and complete identification with guilt that is offered by any art whatsoever. The dynamics of tragic plot correspond to the urgency of our quest for innocence. The passion of tragic eloquence corresponds to the urgency of our plea for a verdict of Not Guilty.' (Bentley 1965 p.261)

While discussing the characteristics and focus of tragedy, something brief has to be said about Freud's deterministic, pessimistic, and tragic; for the individual; ideas. It is easy to see this in the way many versions/performances of Hamlet have opted for an 'Oedipus complex' approach; fixated on his mother, difficult relations with other women and his father (power issues), and a tendency to focus on Hamlet as the repressed and psychologically isolated Bourgeois man, rather than place him in to a set of socio-political contexts of his role in the Danish royalty, society and given his university education etcetera, civilisation, at that time. Focusing on the tragically isolated, repressed, and tormented soul character, misses the point about being a social being striving to find the necessary actions for resolution.

'...we must understand capitalist society not only in terms of economic and political oppression, but also as involving the psychic oppression and emotional impoverishment of the individual who, through the inculcation of guilt, is an active participant in her or his own subordination to the imperatives of the social system as a whole.' (Leonard 1984 p. 41)

Using the tragic form of drama in TV, then and now

'Tragedy, said Aristotle, is the "imitation of noble actions", and though it is some twenty-five hundred years since the dictum was uttered there is only one respect in which we are inclined to modify it. To us "imitation" seems a rather naïve word to apply to that process by which observation is turned into art, and we seek one which would define or at least imply the nature of that interposition of the personality of the artist between the object and the beholder which constitutes his function.' (Krutch 1929 p.870/1)

Krutch argues that in the modern world the word 'expression' would fit more easily than 'imitation' in our understanding of the way in which the artist transforms 'observation' in to dramatic form. The dramatist wants to venture off in to some expression of this or that account of the human condition under certain circumstances, under pressure. However, that artist must also offer links between this artistic 'expression', in whatever form/medium it is presented, and the 'audience'. Hence the importance of the Prologue and Epilogue in Shakespeare for example, to draw the audience back in, and break the spell of the acting out of drama they are about to experience, or have seen.

In our era, this experience is very likely to be via popular culture? And along the way I will need to consider the other 'ims' to complement Raymond Williams' list cited above, that both give some context to 'our' current predicament, why we are who we are, and where we are, but also help to explain why our artistic 'expressions', and interpretive reception of these creations is more complicated.

Drama is expressive culture, and communication and contact are high on the agenda of all involved with performance. The social-interactions taking place, on the stage or screen, in the theatre or cinema, are complex, many and various. What actors put in to a performance, and an audience, in all its variety, takes out, will clearly matter to all participants whose goals in attending this performance will vary. Reflexivity is a key concept here in our understanding of the conditions of practice of actors. Reflexivity can be understood to be a doubling-back, or self-reference by performers, an on-going reflection on how that performance is going, are the aims of the actor in performing the role achieved?

This is what I would call 'making sense of ourselves', a psycho-social process where 'actors' become self-aware reflectors in action.

Of course the writer(s) and director will also have a view about this; aims and achievement. The actor is required to be another person, and to act out the performance of that person, whoever, and however they are in the story. The actor's presentation of self as someone else masks who that actor actually is, and of course the actor, other actors, writer, director, audience member, critics and so on, will have a view about how effectively an actor has performed that task. Has the actor displayed communicative competence in this role playing? This question is probably most important for the actor their self in this reflexive way. Some roles; and Shakespeare is an example here; require the actor/character being played, to break the 'barrier', the 'fourth wall', between the stage and the audience, by offering an aside to the audience, drawing them in to the action, co-conspirators.

The motives of all participants will be there in the inter-action of performance whether this is evident, transparent, or not. All those involved in performing a tragedy, conveying tragic characters in tragic, unfolding events, cannot fail to reflect upon this. We do this in our everyday lives, but, the very manner of drama, the deliberate concentration of life's rich tapestry in a specific time and space sharpens our engagement. The intent of all engaged in the drama, are also involved in the social production of meaning. So, for participants in the drama, narrative takes the lead, an aspect of the way telling stories enables us to make sense of the world and the tragic events and characters that are part of that world. Arnold Wesker once said that words are like bridges, the more words you know, the more places you can go to. But, whose stories are being told, and by whom for what purposes?

Popular culture has both the reach, and the potential audience, but also attracts the creative energies of many escapees, those 'artists' who have raised their consciousness of the everyday paradox that is life? This good news of a hope in the future, and the opportunity, necessity even, for ordinary people to take responsibility for change, to be agents of change, is the message? And, from 'our' lofty heights of 'serious art', reserved for a minority of cultured types, we need to make the best of engagement with/within popular culture to expose for all to see the intolerable, barbaric, and socially unjust world in which we live?

But, as discussed elsewhere in this essay, the label of 'elitism' is often still attached to art forms like theatre;

'But to call theatre "elitist" is only justified if the work seeks to obscure rather than illuminate, if the actors are reluctant to communicate, or if the theatre repels a potential audience through excessively high prices or a selectively exclusive attitude to the public.' (Eyre & Wright 2000 p.320)

As Eyre and Wright go on to say the term 'popular theatre' is used to describe very different productions ranging from a left-wing political offering to mass audience West End musicals etcetera.

And, given that there has been endless, and invariably pessimistic, comment that traditional forms of Tragedy; the Greeks, Shakespeare and so on, are not now viable in our (post) modern world, all the more reason to embrace the possibilities that contemporary popular culture, has and does offer us. However, we know that the modern world comes with a wide range of issues associated with the economics of everyday life, and how increasingly our actions, and inter-actions, are contextualised by money.

Grayson Perry, the artist and BAFTA awarded TV programme maker, has emphasised the basic money related aspects of art;

'There are two metrics that carry weight in the art world. One is auction price: how much in cold cash someone is prepared to pay for a particular piece by a particular artist. The other is visitor figures: how many people go to see certain exhibitions. Some artists have often taken the self-designated moral high ground by claiming not to care about either of these measurements of success. Art for them exists on some inhuman, ethereal plane with no need for an audience, or money. I'm not one of them.' (Perry 2017)

In his 2013 Reith lectures; 'written up' in his 2014 book 'Playing to the Gallery', he sought to develop the argument of his TV programmes about 'the vanity of small differences', i.e. what is there in our engagement with art that can be used as a status symbol in the endless 'snakes and ladders' jostling?

'This assertion of identity through cultural choices is tricky, because what is exclusive and what is popular constantly shifts. One minute we feel we are on the cutting edge of taste; the next all our consumer choices seem very predictable and kitsch. The art critic Clement Greenberg defined kitsch as art after the soul has departed...Art heavyweights sometimes forget they are part of the leisure industry. People, on the whole, come to art exhibitions on their day off. They do not want to feel that they are doing their homework. Maybe it is time to take the sting out of the word popular.' (Perry 2017)

When he won the highly prestigious Turner Prize in 2003, Perry immediately set about changing (even lowering?) the tone by declaring that it was about time that a transvestite potter received the award.

However, these 'culture wars' are by no means new. The 1960s era of working class oriented literature and drama (amongst other practices) reflected these cultural confrontations, for example in the work of David Storey, David Mercer, Alan Sillitoe, and Shelagh Delaney amongst others, where the creators of these stories about the human condition were offering up their own 'rags to riches' story of development from their origins to destinations of successful middle class-ness. Stories of the uncompleted transition from a working class family life to an artistic freedom, and psychological ambiguity. All these contributions contributed to a new wave of social realism.

As mentioned earlier one well known example of TV drama that truly caused widespread consternation was the broadcast of Jeremy Sandford's play 'Cathy Come Home' in November 1966 on BBC1. The TV drama, and most certainly a tragedy, produced by Tony Garnett and directed by Ken Loach (and they were to become a prolific and creative duo), caused questions to be asked in Parliament which reflected the liberal middle class shock that this sort of thing was still happening. Coincidentally, Shelter the homelessness charity, whose creators were in the know, had just been started.

The screening of this play was also a contribution to what is generally regarded as a 'golden age' of UK TV drama which I mentioned earlier, with the BBC and ITV vying for who could commission the best writers, and draw the biggest audiences.

In his book on TV drama Caughie suggests caution regarding the designation 'golden ages', because, obviously, this accolade tends to be 'awarded' some time later. But, as I argue generally, many of the protagonists; writers, producers and directors, knew they were breaking new ground, and had a mission to fulfil. However, As Caughie says;

'In television drama, the day-to-day experience of the people involved was probably much as professional life always is; a mixture of satisfactions and frustrations, victories and defeats, bureaucratic hassles and creative surprises, moments of excitement punctuating long stretches of routine.' (Caughie 2000 p.57)

Tony Garnett in his production role at the BBC would often need to devise ways of getting projects and budgets past the 'bureaucrats', but most of the producers across the TV companies acknowledge some 'battles' were won, and some lost. Delays in premiers was commonplace if there was any hint of controversy, and second showings could be put off or cancelled if reactions went badly.

For all the personnel involved in getting productions to the screen these complexities were part of their conditions of practice, affecting what they did and how they did it.

I can see a clear resemblance here between Orwell's characterisation of a 'decent' ordinary English person, usually rooting for the under-dog, with the enthusiasms of the new era of radicals in TV drama on a varying spectrum of left-wing-ness. Once again we should avoid seeing this new generation of drama creatives as a homogeneous group, they were not. Many tensions existed between the Oxbridge education personnel; writers, producers and directors, who tended to be anti-authoritarian, and those who were not well educated in this formal way, and were more comfortable with a commercially successful approach.

One example of these tensions was the arrival in the UK from Canadian TV of Sydney Newman, employed by ABC TV for Armchair theatre. Most of the drama people I have already cited did know the theatrical canon, they were transforming themselves, and hopefully their audiences, from a well versed dramatic knowledge base set of values. Newman did not, and this did create some significant differences of opinion, especially when he was recruited by the BBC in 1963. Many dramatists believed that this appointment by the BBC said more about the old style BBC patrician values than Newman's commitment to a more social democratic agenda.

In 1960 David Mercer commented on this sedate, almost senior civil service feel, to the BBC drama production management, when he submitted his first play for TV; 'Where the Difference Begins'.

Newman decided to 'upgrade' the single play format to equal billing with series' and serials. In October 1964 'The Wednesday Play' was launched, and became a major contribution to that 'golden age' of TV drama. As mentioned elsewhere one aspect of Newman's democratisation could be seen as his team approach to creating the drama output, with producers, writers and directors, working more closely.

In response to the Newman reforms, the Oxbridge element in BBC drama expressed not only a certain snobbery, but also reinforced the issue of them being located in a values and lifestyle position somewhere between their humbler origins and their recent destinations. However, there seems little doubt that the success of 'The Wednesday Play' raised TV drama to the continuously desired 'seriousness' status. A reputation that fuelled 'the golden age' accolade.

However, as Madeleine MacMurraugh-Kavanagh argues in Janet Thumin's edited book, we should be aware that in internal conflicts within the BBC were a major factor of both continuity and change in both dominant values and output;

'...it becomes clear that whatever claims are made for the "Golden Age" of writer-led drama and BBC innovation as emblematized in The Wednesday Play's groundbreaking triumphs and controversies of the 1964-1970 period. All are based on misconceptions deriving from a failure to inspect and interpret the contemporary evidence...the BBC's relationship with its drama "flagship" The Wednesday Play was, in fact, a great deal more complex, and its interventions more motivated, than official accounts and critical commentaries have previously led us to believe.' (Thumin [Ed.] 2002 p.162)

The BBC managements' politically induced obsession with audience/viewing figures was as major an issue then as it is still today.

Certainly calling this period of the 60s and 70s a golden one should be set within the context of the election of the Thatcher government in 1979.

Attitudes and actions changed, and with less opportunities to create the same dramas. The political climate had changed, with more intervention in terms of what, and who, should be creating TV drama. The moral high-ground benchmark setters and 'bean counters' had established a cultural dominance that was reinforced by the Blair/Brown era after 1997, when everything had to be accounted for, and required to show the return on economic investment. The 'Culture Wars' showed no likelihood of going away! Oppositional values and goals have always existed in the arts, as elsewhere, in the UK, and usually kept at arms-length by the exercise of power and control by the privileged elite. However, once forms of communication are developed and democratised, those 'guardians' of traditional values are very likely to lose their grip on matters. Residual and emergent cultures will find a way in, and begin to remake the world in their own image.

However, with regard to the 1960s, it has to be said that by 1967 the Establishment dominance of the BBC was already changing course, with for example PM Harold Wilson appointing the Tory peer, Lord Hill as chairman of the Corporation. The 'golden age' was effectively over, and in 1969 Hugh Greene, the BBC Director General resigned. Like most frontline, and traditional institutions in the UK, the BBC was run by middle class white men for middle class white men and their wives. As I have already suggested the increasing opposition to that cultural dominance throughout everyday life in society, the demand for a greater open-ness and a plurality of power over policy and practice making was bound to reach even the BBC.

Both before, and after the 1979 phases of TV drama production, is classic Dennis Potter land. Potter wrote a succession of outstanding plays for a 'mass' audience. A key issue referred to by Raymond Williams, discussing television in the late 1950s and 1960s.

'...at certain levels the whole situation of drama has already been transformed. What had ordinarily been, in the theatres, a minority art, was now a major public form.' (Williams 1974 p.58/9)

Some more welcomed by critics and 'censors' than others. When asked about the inter-relation between the theatre stage and TV, and why his preference seemed to be the latter, Potter responded by pointing out the size of the TV audience in comparison to the theatre. Potter was always an enthusiastic advocate for TV drama, emphasising the reflective and educational aspects that the medium could offer, engaging a new generation of creators, and consumers. As I have already said Potter and his contemporaries sought an artistic vehicle that insisted on connection, creating agencies for change, building and using bridges rather than even more symbolic cul-de-sacs.

John Russell Taylor in his 1962 book, 'Anger and After: A guide to the new British drama', emphasises how the playwrights, Osborne et al, were young, more likely working class, and writing for theatres that were opening up to a much more declasse audience.

But despite this 'new' theatre, including the work of Greenwood and McGrath mentioned earlier, the theatre was still primarily divided between the traditional canon of the minority 'serious' drama of Shakespeare, Ibsen, Chekhov etcetera, and the commercial theatre of London's West End and most regional theatres. So, just at the time when a new, more everyday 'realistic' drama was making a case for greater influence, this desire and demand for something radically different was reflected even more so on TV.

Before saying more about Potter, I need to focus on an issue that has been bubbling away beneath the surface of my argument since page 1. TV watching is a near universal leisure pursuit in the UK. Of course people are selective, and watch different channels, usually out of habit. Once people have settled in to their routine of watching TV they are still exposed to some variety, some surprises, that they may or may not like. But watching TV does remain both pleasurable and offer sentimental release. We know from the many reports that have been done in last decade or so that most people (who conventionally watch TV) do not engage with out of the home 'arts'. They rarely go to the cinema, theatre, art galleries, literature and poetry events and so on. So, what value do people place upon 'the arts'? There have been endless arguments about why people are excluded, or, self-exclude themselves from these experiences. Educational experience, formal and informal (community education etcetera) does play in key role in how people orientate themselves to 'the arts'. How curious are people about what these arts experiences have to offer outside of their domestic domain, and even outside of their educational experience and awareness of 'the arts'? Are they interested, can they be bothered, do their values, and particularly, the value placed upon 'the arts' mean that even if they were to engage, they do not have a working knowledge of the arts providers, organisations, and events, that would encourage them to cross the threshold? The cultural capital that they have does not include these assets. The outreach work used by arts organisations to encourage people to engage do not work, people stay at home and watch TV. Where they remain a crucial target audience, especially so for advertising.

Earlier on in this essay a cited Raymond Williams on Modern Tragedy, with his emphasis on how critiques of modern life have been influenced by Marxism, Freudianism and Existentialism. The shaping of Dennis Potter's world view, and the context for his extensive, ground breaking drama output, embraces all three!

Fans of Potter's work will know very well that he drew heavily on his own childhood, and later illness, to craft his TV plays. He mined his own life to approach and connect up with his audience. One of major later works, 'The Singing Detective' is a good example of this idea; reflection on the self, hangups about parents, especially so fathers, use of fantasy and the singular role of imaginative connections with his audiences own fantasies and imagination, are key to his dramatic, and tragic, output. One significant aspect of the fantasy element of which both 'Pennies from Heaven' and 'The Singing Detective' are prime examples was the manner in which his characters would suddenly break from the dialogue and burst in to song! Plus, the manner of this evoked strong emotional and cultural connections for the audience as the actors mimed to songs from the period of the action, drawn up from the popular musical cultural 'archive'.

Potter was attracted by the dark parts of the forest, literally and metaphorically. His TV play 'Blue Remembered Hills', where adult actors played the role of children, was a good example of this. And, there was tragedy here. Earlier in this essay I cited Karl Manheim's book 'Ideology and Utopia', about the fictions and the wish-dreams, that add up to the utopias that people create for themselves. Potter's work is very much about this, in the way he sought to show complexity in people and their lives, and avoid stereotypes. Fantasy and reality inter-acting on the screen and with the audience.

Potter understood that the course of the journey from the past to the present, and beyond, is not a neat straight line. There are always ruptures in these timescales, with for example two different time scales operating simultaneously in 'The Singing Detective'; which one can you trust? The notion of ruptures in time and narrative is to found in most of Potter's work, along with many other Modernist writers and artists of all kinds. He wanted to tell his audience not to trust 'official' accounts of the past, to be wary about top-down stories about progress. He, like others, challenges the 'shop-soiled' moralism that is trotted out by the media on a daily basis. Like many Modernists, (and increasingly 'post-modernists) and certainly many of those who made up 'the golden age', he distrusted language to tell the truth, hence the concentration on the image, and the song/music. Contrary to conventional TV, Potter deliberately disorientates the viewer. The abstract world that usually defies a simple, hackneyed, explanation. We are forced to think again about the veracity of what we believe we know. The past, memories, may need to be re-assessed? This is most certainly true of Potter's final pairing of dramas, 'Karaoke' and 'Cold Lazarus', shown on both the BBC and Channel 4 after his death.

Potter died in June 1994, and on the day of his death the BBC aired a special celebratory programme about his life and work. In that programme he was referred to as equal of Bernard Shaw, and the George Orwell that society still needed. The need has not gone away.

The 2006 BBC4 documentary 'Left of Frame: the rise and fall of radical TV drama' focused on these issues emphasising the way in which a number of politically left wing writers (like Jim Allen), producers (like Tony Garnett) and directors (like Ken Loach) made a series of plays that sought to tell stories; historical and contemporary, about working class lives and the struggle for a decent life at home and at work. The documentary featured several writers who emphasised that they were not personally particularly interested in party politics, but concerned with the general condition of politics in society. Many of the plays were not overtly political in a party political way, but the subject matter was certainly political in that they raised a series of issues about the oppression and repression commonly experienced by ordinary working people in their everyday lives. The plays sought to challenge conventional opinions.

This approach was matched by a good deal of 'censorship' through, for example, 'blacklisting' certain writers. It was always alleged that the BBC had internal monitoring of 'political' people, whose files were marked with a code to indicate that they should not be offered contracts.

Ken Loach reflected on the changes over the years from the 1960s to the 80s by suggesting that the earlier TV audience were more innocent, and therefore viewed the TV plays through different eyes. By the 1980s the TV drama audience had become used to what TV could offer, and had incorporated the Soap Opera form of TV (melo)drama, The advent of Channel 4 had expanded the Soap Opera viewing options via Brookside, which consistently showed drama written by radical playwrights of the 60s and 70s era.

The 'structure of feeling' that I mentioned earlier incorporated the fact that many of this new generation of 'dramatists' experienced higher education at an Oxbridge college, the usual fertile ground for BBC recruitment. Indeed, many were there on scholarships, who, rather than conforming to, and reinforcing the cultural and social status quo, rebelled against it; rebels most definitely with a cause! Also many also reflected upon, and put on the TV screen, the unease they felt, caught between their working class and lower middle class background, and their new 'liberated' self. Potter's 'Nigel Barton' plays summed this up very well.

Many of the features of these past years of politically motivated TV drama; working class life as the subject matter, writers, and production values, were present in the 1996 BBC TV series 'Our Friends in the North', written by Peter Flannery, and adapted for TV from an earlier RSC stage production. The serial's historical span was from 1964 with the election of the Labour government lead by Harold Wilson, to the election of Margaret Thatcher in 1979.

Writing notes in 2002 for the DVD collection he says;

'It's over 20 years since I began to write a story about four young people growing up in post-war Britain. I was resident writer at the Royal Shakespeare Company, so I had absorbed a lot of big plays that chronicled the state of the nation…I think the drama serial was really one of Britain's greatest cultural inventions in the last century. It is now all but eclipsed by the series form – the long runners and the soaps; drama that refuses to end. It's like watching loads of talented writers, actors, producers, and tv executives who appear to have contracted Alzheimer's and forgotten that they've already said and done all this. To be useful to an audience, a story has to end. It's the basic duty of a story.' (Flannery 2002)

On reading these liner notes for the first time I was reminded of Marx's comments on history repeating itself in his essay on mid nineteenth century French politics;

'Hegel remarks somewhere that all facts and personages of great importance in world history occur, as it were, twice. He forgot to add: the first time as tragedy, the second as farce...Men make their own history, but they do not make it under circumstances chosen by themselves, but under circumstances directly encountered, give and transmitted from the past.' (Marx 1869)

Hannah Arendt discussed the repetition of tragic events through which 'the hero' comes to understand the situation, even has an epiphany as an aspect of this recognition and realisation?

Flannery's characters, especially the most overtly politically conflicted Nicky Hutchinson, exemplify this reading of the drawing on, and eventual personal and social collisions with, the past. For example, Nicky and his teenage sweetheart, Mary Soulsby, are the first persons from their working class families to attend university. They appear to have broken the cultural mould only for their pasts to catch up with, and dis-rail their plans.

A present day equivalent would be Liverpool's Jimmy McGovern, dramatist and TV plays writer; for example, 'Cracker', 'The Street', and 'The Accused'. He has been a regular critic of snobbery associated with the choice of medium to convey a social realism oriented drama.

He raises key high/low culture issues; for example, on who decides on these values? He also criticises the role of commissioning executives in TV who according to McGovern still feel they know best about programming, what the working class like and want see on their TV screens. This leads, he argues, to repetition in programming, repeating the same formula. Theirs is a 'top down' view of everyday life, and not written by working class people themselves as a creative process exploring aspects of their own lives and problems. For McGovern, being 'close' to the subject matter stands a much greater chance of conveying something approaching a real life of laughter and tears. For McGovern, the point of the drama should be in the story actually being told.

In recent years Steve McQueen has been doing the same with regard to the lives led by black people in the U.K., telling the untold stories, a different, grass roots, social history. In addition to his films made for cinema, for example 'Shame' and 'Twelve Years a Slave', he has written for television, with his 2020 BBC series 'Small Axe'. McQueen has said that this series a very personal project reflecting his own life and the community in which he lived, went to school, and so on. An insider's view of that world.

Writing now, in August 2021, marks the tenth anniversary of the 'riots' that swept across England. Another film maker Baff Akoto was the focus of a Guardian article by Jack Shenker (7.8.21.);

'Akoto's work could be interpreted as a provocative intervention in the so-called "culture wars", but he's keen to resist that framing. "You hope there's something timeless about a piece of art," he says. "The great challenge is to make something that can withstand the incessant waves of topicality, and when all is said and done still matter in some way." Part of the timelessness in this case may lie in the fact that, far from disappearing, in many parts of the UK the conditions that helped produce the events of August 2011 – from tensions over policing, to economic exclusion – have intensified.'

One further issue to be raised here in the media's obsession with topicality, is an enthusiasm with creating heroes; but looked at rationally on a very spurious set of criteria of what would actually amount to heroic acts. It is also the case of a hero today, but fallen from grace tomorrow, and often the 'strawman' effect; set them up to create another media moment in knocking them down again. But topicality is central to television, certainly so with 'Soaps', where the audience are offered the continuance of the everyday life of characters alongside their own everyday lives, a shared quotidian, but still with that openness of the uncompleted nature of the story. Audience members talk to each other about the narrative of television drama, especially so 'Soaps', they bring their understandings to this conversation. So, while the world is spinning, and the unresolved issues of change accumulates over time, the television version of everyday life offers continuity.

What I should also say now is that the role of Tragedy as a viable, suitable, vehicle for telling (those) stories about our lives, has been questioned, and even regarded as out of date, and no longer suitable. But, I would argue that given the trajectory of actual life in twenty-first century (post)modernity, we may dismiss Tragedy from the shiny front door only for it to return by a deliberately obscured back door!

TV drama as Tragedy;
'Unforgotten' as a case study

A Tragedy will certainly depict tragic events and characters, often, paradoxically, for our entertainment. I thought about this a good deal while watching through, and thoroughly enjoying, the four series of 'Unforgotten', written by Chris Lang, directed by Andy Wilson, produced by Tim Bradley, and acted out by a stellar cast lead by Nicola Walker (Cassie) and Sanjeev Bhaskar (Sunny). These plays emphasised for me just how good mainstream TV can be given the right combination of people and insightful commissioning.

What I wish to say here as a concrete example of my theme is why I believe that 'Unforgotten' was an excellent example of Tragedy, and why this is important for us culturally and politically. This is popular culture (i.e. created and produced for a large and diverse audience with considerable variations in educational background) at its best, and sadly stands in stark contrast to 90% plus of contemporary TV which is both vulgar and banal. Good products of popular culture are entertaining, stirring, demandingly thought-provoking, and essentially, educational. They are educational because they encourage us to think about the experiences portrayed in the drama, even discuss them, and also consider how what we have watched tells us something important about, gives us insight in to, the human condition. Who are we? What are we like? What values do we hold? Values that direct our attitudes and actions, our inter-relations with others; who do we care about? what do we care about? what is unique about us as a person? what do we share with others, near and far? The great variety of forms that is popular culture can offer real, and timely opportunities for creativity, enlightenment, understanding and social solidarity. An insight in to tragedy, from TV or elsewhere, helps us to incorporate these events in to our everyday experience, emphasising that this could happen to any of us given a certain set of circumstances.

In Series 2 of 'Unforgotten' three lead characters; all suspected of murder;

68

are in fact the victims of sexual abuse in their childhoods. The story reveals and plays out the appalling consequences of the secrets, lies and heartbreak that follows from this experience. We witness three 'good' people; one a school teacher, one a cancer nurse, and the third a barrister doing a lot of free work for needy clients. Their work is clearly virtuous, and yet?

There is redemption for these characters because Cassie and Sunny can see it would be wrong to punish them further, to take away their hope for a better life.

As Eagleton says;

'What makes for tragedy, often enough, is exactly the fact that we can indeed conceive of a more humane condition' (Eagleton 2008 p.344)

And indeed what he goes on to emphasise is echoed in my comments about raised hopes and disappointments;

'The immense political scandal of our world is that things could be feasibly a good deal better than they are. The red herring of utopian perfection is cynically intended among other things, to distract us from the outrage.

...Similarly, it is the lesson of a good deal of tragedy that only by an unutterably painful openness to our frailty and finitude – to the material limits of our condition – can we have any hope of transcending it.' (Eagleton 2008 p.344/45)

In this essay I have consistently raised the question of the way TV, along with other media, has been used in conventional ways, perhaps as a form of social control. I have argued that we need to look carefully at the way TV content etcetera, has been responded to by the growing audience. People have not always been 'amusing themselves to death', but actually challenging the form and content of TV programming, the dominant values that underpin choices, scheduling, subject matter, and production.

In an analysis of the 1960s and beyond, a great deal has been made of the 'active consumption' of working people, especially so in their engagement with new forms of popular culture like rock/pop music and TV. The belief that the working class only had American influenced popular, i.e. low-culture, entertainments foisted upon them, take it or leave it, was being challenged. More was being made of the buying power and aesthetic judgements being made by the younger generation in particular (my generation!). It was argued that there was a shift from an orchestrated supply determining demand situation, to one of demand determining supply. This was like my reference to Edward Thompson's argument discussed above, of a 're-making' of the young working class (with some young middle class fellow-travellers); they now had agency, and were calling the cultural shots. These new freedoms, these cultural choices, reflected the shifts in British society which I sketched out at the start of this essay. Some critics went even further to argue that this youthful seizing of control over the direction of culture represented a significant attack upon the hegemony of the traditional cultural elites in society.

I have already argued in this essay that I do not believe that this 'pop/popular culture' moment had much lasting effect on power relations in society, and, for example, that the culture production corporations maintained, and then increased their stranglehold over production and consumption. The enduring power of the ICAs, and as already addressed the daily control and manipulation of social communications;

'It is a Marxist commonplace that all social communication is ideologically inflected, a psychoanalytic one that all conscious communication is in part unconsciously determined. A development as well as a critique of these positions is Foucault's claim that any discourse is a power-knowledge relationship.' (Wolfenstein 1993 p.96)

This is a concern with which Stuart Laing concludes his 1986 book, 'Representations of Working-Class Life 1957 – 1964.' Taking up the issue of attempting an evaluation of the relations between media content and the audience, assessing the manner of changes, he says;

'At the same time such assessment would need to judge the value of a cultural practice which is committed, in ways which cut across conventional divisions between "serious" and the "popular", to the representation of contemporary social experience in terms which can offer denials and alternatives to dominant forms of generalised social description. In such an assessment the apportioning of praise or blame is ultimately less important than to learn and to judge what is possible and what is necessary for our own contemporary cultural practice.' (Laing 1986 p.223)

One of the key issues I have to address in this essay is whether the positive claims I make for the value of TV drama as one aspect of an invigorated and transformative popular culture, actually stands up to scrutiny. Is the TV audience, now, ready for both more one-off plays, and for tragic scenarios that consider our present imperfect times; for example, more isolation of people and places, greater poverty on a world scale, greater inequality at home, a loss of belief in parliamentary democracy and party politics, and so on?

Is the current greater diversity in cultural and aesthetic awareness, and practice, reflective of a younger generation campaigning against the paradoxes of conventional obsessions with economic growth and climate crisis, with sexism, racism, nationalism, rampant globalisation concentrated in fewer, richer, hands, going to make a difference to what people demand to see on their TV screens?

A Conclusion

Writing this essay has allowed me to reflect upon several issues that have been of concern to me for some time. Being a sociologist of culture has resulted in a good deal of research, writing, course creation and teaching over many years. Being a Critical Theorist has also meant that when looking at 'art', for self and society in the widest sense, I have highlighted the economic, political, social and cultural inequalities that dominate UK society. As a devotee of William Morris, I have followed his demands that access to engaging with, and working in, 'the arts' should be open to all. Not the least of our demands is that those in society who are rich and powerful should not determine aesthetic criteria nor control what is of value, monetarily or otherwise.

I have also been keen to advocate the educational role of the arts, including wider aspects of the media including broadcasting. I have touched on these issues in this essay, and emphasised that TV in particular as one dimension of popular culture has often been, and could be so much more, a valuable educational vehicle for greater enlightenment, and pleasure. I have argued the case that the role of TV drama in particular in our everyday lives could contribute a great deal more to people of all backgrounds in coming to understand, and work through, the complexities and paradoxes of life, and our own roles as a part of it.

As I write, the current government like many before it, are attempting to undermine public sector broadcasting, with a view to breaking it up, asset stripping, and selling off to their avaricious friends what they all consider to be the best money making portions. This situation is not helped by the behaviour of the elite liberal establishment, who will rub their hands in the usual angst ridden way, while not actually confronting the money obsessed people who have a stranglehold on so many people's lives.

As I have said in this essay there are some very good examples of 'TV' drama created by subscription media organisations like Netflix. But, despite their growth in confidence and the reach that they have, still do not match the much fuller range of terrestrial TVs offering, in the past (and often archived), currently, and hopefully in the future. At this time, it is good to see that the BBC are engaging in a self-promotion campaign that is both well overdue and very necessary. C4 and ITV companies could also do much more to enhance the reputation of public sector broadcasting. We need proselytizers, now. Even if we are lying in the gutter it is possible to look up at the stars!

All of us in the UK who believe that TV still has a lot to offer that is educational, informational and entertaining, should be taking more responsibility. We could all be advocating a role for broadcasting (as radio has a key role to play) that will enhance people's lives, give them a voice through vocation and engagement, and promote ideas about using their agency for change.

Tragedy in our everyday lives
Bibliography

Astley, John 2008 *'Herbivores & Carnivores: the struggle for democratic cultural values in post-war Britain.'*

Bennett et al (Eds) 1981 *'Culture, Ideology and Social Processes'*

Bentley, Eric 1965 *'The Life of the Drama'*

Bragg, Melvyn 2010 *'The South Bank Show: Final Cut.'*

Caughie, John 2000 *'Television Drama: Realism, Modernism and British Culture'*

Cohen, Anthony P 1985 *'The Symbolic Construction of Community.'*

Dukore, Bernard F. 1974 (Ed.) *'Dramatic Theory and Criticism'*

Eagleton, Terry 2003 *'Sweet Violence: The Idea of the Tragic'*

Edgar, David 1988 *'The Second Time as Farce: Reflections on the Drama of Mean Times.'*

Elliott, Larry and Atkinson, Dan 2007 *'Fantasy Island: Waking up to the incredible economic, political and social illusions of the Blair legacy.'*

Ellis, John 2000 *'Seeing Things: Television in the age of uncertainty'*

Ellis, John 1999 *'Television as working-through'* in Gripsrud (Ed)

Eyre, Richard & Wright, Nicholas 2000 *'Changing Stages: A view of British theatre in the twentieth century'*

75

Felski, Rita 2008 (Ed.) *'Rethinking Tragedy'*

Flannery, Peter 2002 Liner notes for the DVD version of *'Our Friends in the North'.*

Gray, Ann and McGuigan, Jim (Eds) 1993 *'Studying Culture: An Introductory Reader'*

Gripsrud, Jostein (Ed) 1999 *'Television and Common Knowledge'*

Hall, Stuart and Whannel, Paddy 1964 *'The Popular Arts'*

Hall, Stuart 1988 *'The Hard Road to Renewal'*

Hartnoll, Phyllis 1968 *'The Theatre: A concise history'*

Hewison, Robert 2014 *'Cultural Capital: The rise and fall of creative Britain'*

Kohon, Gregorio (Ed) 1986 *'The British school of psychoanalysis: The Independent tradition'*

Krutch, Joseph 1929 *'The Tragic Fallacy'* in Dukore

Laing, Stuart 1986 *'Representations of Working-Class Life 1957 – 1964'*

Lefebvre, Henri 1968 *'Everyday Life in the Modern World'*

Leonard, Peter 1984 *'Personality and Ideology'*

Marx, Karl 1869 (first published in English in 1934) *'The Eighteenth Brumaire of Louis Bonaparte'.*

Mulgan, Geoff 1996 *'Culture: The problem with being public'* in Marquand,

David and Seldon, Anthony (Eds) *'The Ideas that shaped post-war Britain.'*

Mulvey, L. and Sexton, J. (Eds) 2007 *'Experimental British Television'*

Murdock, Graham 1999 *'Rights and Representations: Public discourse and cultural citizenship'* in Gripsrud (Ed)

Nelson, Robin 2007 *'State of Play: Contemporary "high-end" TV drama'*

Perry, Grayson *'Popular is not a dirty word'* The Guardian 27 May 2017

Samuel, Raphael (Ed) 1981 *'People's History and Socialist Theory'*

Sandhu, Sukhdev 2021 The Guardian Review 14.8.21 *'In praise of a vanished age in British TV…'*

Silverstone, Roger 1994 *'Television and everyday life'*

Sinfield, Alan 1989 *'Literature, Politics and Culture in Postwar Britain.'*

Steiner, George *1961 'The Death of Tragedy'*

Stevenson, Nick 1997 *'Media, Ethics and Morality'* in McGuigan, Jim (Ed) of *'Cultural Methodologies'*

Taylor, John Russell 1962 *'Anger and After'*

Thumin, Janet (Ed) *'Small Screens, Big Ideas: Television in the 1950s'*

Williams, Raymond *1974 'Television: Technology and Cultural Form.'*

Williams, Raymond 1979 *'Modern Tragedy'*

Wolfenstein, Eugene Victor 1993 *'Psychoanalytic-marxism'*

Young, Rob 2021 *'The Magic Box: Viewing Britain through the Rectangular Window'*